The Expo Celebration

The Official Retrospective Book

EXPO 86

**The 1986
World Exposition**
Vancouver
British Columbia
May 2 – October 13, 1986

The tradition of Kodak and world expositions is over a hundred years stong. As a corporate participant at EXPO 86, we were pleased to sponsor the much-photographed Kodak Pacific Bowl, home of the RCMP Musical Ride, and the Kodak International Nights of Fire, the nightly spectacular of fireworks and lasers choreographed to original music. No more fitting way can be found to crown our involvement at Expo than in this book.

As sponsor of *The Expo Celebration* we are proud to have the exposition remembered with these photographs. Kodachrome film and Ektachrome film were used exclusively on all assignments, the same high quality film many of the 20 million visitors used to capture their own special memories. Kodak was proud to have been involved in the 1986 World Exposition and know that you'll treasure your copy of its photographic retrospective; *The Expo Celebration.*

Kodak

The Expo Celebration is dedicated to
the people of British Columbia and
to wheelchair athlete Rick Hansen's
Man in Motion World Tour. Rick
believes in a dream. We, too, believe
that dreams can come true.

Copyright ©
Murray/Love Productions Inc.
1128 Homer Street
Vancouver, B.C., Canada
V6B 2X6

Published by:
Whitecap Books Ltd.
1086 West 3rd Street
North Vancouver, B.C., Canada
V7P 3J6

The Expo Celebration
Creative Director/Photo Editor: Derik Murray
Director of Operations: Marthe Love
Director of Marketing/Production: Michael Burch
Photography Coordinator: Michael Morissette
Designer: Ray Hrynkow
Interviewer/Writer: David Grierson

The Expo Celebration was printed by Agency Press,
with typesetting by The Typeworks,
dustjacket and introductory pages by Slicko Studios,
colour separations by Zenith Graphics,
binding by Northwest Bindery, printed on Provincial
Papers-Jensen Gloss 200 M.

Printed and bound in British Columbia, Canada.

ISBN 0-921061-01-3

CONTENTS

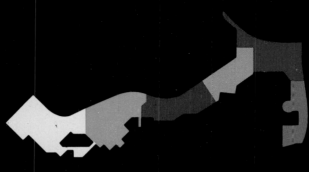

VISION

In the summer of 1986 the world came to British Columbia. From near and far they brought the wonders of their technology, culture and people to EXPO 86. In order for this impressive gathering of nations to occur it took the foresight and dedication of a number of people, including the visionaries shown here. Each, through his own position or portfolio, ensured that the 1986 World Exposition would not only come to be, but would be a resounding success. The contributions of these individuals are acknowledged by these excerpts from interviews with them.

Nigel Dickson

"Expo is unique because it combines a number of elements; the technologies of the two areas – transportation and communications – and it also involves the arts and entertainment to a greater degree. That puts the element of fun on the site so that while people are waiting for pavilions, the outside is as much fun as the inside.

"Expo has created a legacy that the people of B.C. feel and I feel when I go on that site. That is, people feel good about themselves, about being British Columbians.

"The Exposition has been educational for British Columbians as to where our future prosperities lie and the international aspects of how that relates to B.C.

"I think they got a sense of a pretty good future."

WILLIAM BENNETT,
Premier – Province of B.C.
(Retired – 1986), Kelowna, B.C.

"It was our intention to present Canada in a magnificent showcase, to reflect the vibrance and the spirit of Canada, particularly the importance of transportation and communication in the evolution of this country. Particularly the leadership that Canada has demonstrated to the world in terms of its achievements.

"I think, in terms of Vancouver being the gateway to the Pacific Rim, that EXPO 86 will go down as a very important event in opening new doors, new opportunities for Canada.

"I can only be reminded of a comment made by an American journalist who visited Expo during the first week and said, 'This is going to be a great show. It's in the right place at the right time and it has the right theme.' I couldn't agree more."

DONALD MAZANKOWSKI,
Deputy Prime Minister/
Minister Responsible for EXPO 86.
Ottawa, Ontario.

Hugh Martell

Hans Sipma

"I'm content enough that it's a family exposition, but it has had to be more than that…to be successful and to make it worthwhile for the nations to have been here. There would be no Exposition without the fifty-four foreign governments in particular and we have to respect that they came here to do a job for their own country. They didn't come here just to be nice to the citizens of Vancouver, although they have been nice and the citizens of Vancouver have responded. The contribution from the nations of the developing world, for example, has been to me the most remarkable of all. The industrialized world can take this theme and work it up in a variety of ways. It's much tougher for the developing countries. Yet they are here in solid enough numbers to represent with honour two-thirds of humanity. Add the solid contribution of the more developed nations, the unity and diversity of the host nation

in a splendid array of government and corporate pavilions – and you have the essential ingredients of a great exposition."

PATRICK REID,
*Ambassador and Commissioner
General – The 1986 World Exposition,
Vancouver, B.C.*

"British Columbia now has a profile it never had before. We've been on every television network, magazines and newspapers around the world. So we now have a recognition factor that just did not exist before. It existed, but not to that degree.

"I think the Exposition will have a lasting impact on British Columbians and Canadians, because they feel good about it. The Exposition's been a success and everybody's proud of it. You can do these things technically correct and bring them in on time and under budget and all that, but if people don't like it, it doesn't matter."

CLAUDE RICHMOND,
*Provincial Minister
Responsible for EXPO 86,
Victoria, B.C.*

Hans Sipma

Tim Harvey

"What do I think about? The attendance. First thing every morning is the attendance. What's it going to be like today? And I check it every hour.

"What Expo does for the province is something the economists, the university professors, the government, the researchers can tell you. My job's to put the Exposition on. I am *one* of the people that helped put the Exposition on.

"There have been 96 Expo Committees formed in the small towns of British Columbia. There have been literally hundreds of projects of which Expo has been the catalyst.

"If there are heroes of this Exposition, they are the volunteers and the people of the small towns of British Columbia who've supported us from day one."

JIM PATTISON,
*Chairman of the Board –
Expo 86 Corporation,
Vancouver, B.C.*

CREATION

Walking the site of EXPO 86, it quickly became evident that a strong cohesive sense of design and purpose underlay the Exposition. For that to become a reality, the top minds in a variety of fields were called upon to make the dream come true.

They called Ron Woodall 'the guru' in the years before Expo opened. As Creative Director he was charged with keeping the creative faith. To acknowledge Mr. Woodall's immense contribution we are pleased to be able to include some of his thoughts on the creative process behind the 1986 World Exposition.

"Nobody designs a world exposition. There's nobody who sits down at a drawing board and draws it. It's done by a series of people. I had a job description when I arrived and it was calling for a very schizophrenic person. Somebody who could deal with all the intangibles and also do an organizational chart and a budget. I guess I had myself cloned and always had somebody to work with me who understood the administrative side of the job.

"Assuming that the experience desired from the Exposition should match what we tried to achieve for the visitors, the experience should be mixed. This sounds very dull. It's learning within a context of fun. You leave one world of the familiar and the commonplace and you walk through the gates into a world where the stimuli are quite different. I don't know that everyone is sensitive to exactly what creates that feeling, part of it is the absence of advertising. We wanted to try and have a look at a set of stimuli in here which were totally different from what you experience on the outside. We've come close to achieving that.

"An exposition is like a salad and you have to have the right amount of anchovies and the right amount of croutons. You're dealing with questions like: How much science centre? How much Disneyland? How much shopping centre? How much national gesture? How much pomp? How much entertainment? What kind of entertainment? It is such a mix. In our case, the decade being what it is – a little depressed, a little cynical, a lot of angst, a lot of problems – we tended toward a kind of celebration.

"Once you have the site laid out, you put in some asphalt, you put in the sewers, you put in the wiring and you put in a couple of buildings. Then someone says, 'we're going to need to put some stuff in here because people are going to come to look at the stuff.' And that's when you get into theming and exhibits and all of that.

"At a personal level, probably the aspect of Expo that upsets me is the number of anonymous contributors. People who really invested their souls for years and then just disappeared, never to be mentioned. Key, key players who are not part of this. The nature is it's like a game of musical chairs. Whoever is standing at the end tends to take the bow. And that's very true of myself. As long as I can continue repeating the message that hundreds of people contributed and as long as I believe that maybe somebody is interested in the specifics of who did what, I'm comfortable symbolically taking the bow. But I wish it was possible to specifically assign credit, assign authorship."

RON WOODALL, *Creative Director – EXPO 86, W. Vancouver, B.C.*

By all accounts, EXPO 86 was a success beyond anyone's wildest dreams. As Mr. Woodall said so eloquently, there were many people whose untiring efforts to make the Exposition possible have gone without acknowledgement. Joining his remarks on this page are remarks made by just a few of the others.

As Vice President of Planning and Development, it was Richard Blagborne's

Alex Waterhouse-Hayward

job to take the seemingly disparate elements of the World Exposition and bring them together on the site in a sense of order, keeping the themed purpose in mind.

"The idea was to add a sub-theme to the theme of transportation and communications, which was called 'a celebration of ingenuity.' That was my byline when I was there. That was what I would always use with every international participant that we talked to. We said, 'Look, what we're talking about here is a celebration of your ingenuity as it relates to transportation and communication. Your ox cart is a wonderful story. Five thousand years of continuous use is a helluva success story. Tell it! It's just as legit as the space shuttle. It's ingenuity! The fundamental idea was that if people could walk away from the Exposition feeling that we're basically pretty ingenious all over the world, and some of that ingenuity is being applied to basically worthwhile endeavours that you'd feel pretty good when you left Expo."

RICHARD BLAGBORNE,
Designer, Vancouver, B.C.

All political considerations aside, the physical location of pavilions, buildings, services, and attractions on the Expo site was a major task. Ian Carter, as Director of Design Services had that responsibility.

"There's a very important rhythm to this site. It runs right down the middle of it. That's the central circulation route which enables one to get from one end of the site to the other, just two miles long. If you compare that circulation route to a

string of pearls, somewhere the pearls are bigger than others. The biggest pearl might be the British Columbia Pavilion complex. But there's always something happening and it's all tied together by that circulation route, which is helped enormously by the monorail. But what is also important, in terms of these pearls, is that one of the most important things on the site is the product base. Where exactly the pavilions are on site. The fact that we have the US at one end, China at the other and Russia in the middle means there are draws all over the site. There very rarely are specific areas on the site where there's a terrific crush of people and an empty space elsewhere."

IAN CARTER,
Architect, Vancouver, B.C.

EXPO 86 was a feast of design and colour. Taking into consideration the successful use of colour at the recent Olympic Games in Los Angeles, the designers and planners of Expo decided to incorporate colour planning into the site right from the beginning. Expo became one of the finest examples of colour planning in recent memory. Robert McIlhargey was hired by Expo to create the plan.

"In the whole colour program for Expo there were only two key colours on the site that were predetermined. The Red Zone was for the Canada Portal which was essentially a Canadian idea, and then the Blue Zone which is the Plaza of Nations, B.C. Pavilion and Expo Headquarters. We had a blue and a red, which set up a warm and cool

combination. From there we were looking for fairly bright chromatic colours that were more akin to what you'd find on racing cars, on airplanes, on boxcars…transportation colours, if you like.

"You start on the west end of the site with yellow, which is warm, then the cool of the green, into the hots of the pinks and cool of the blue, back to red and out to purple on the east end. It wasn't intended to make one area hotter than another. It was just a way of choreographing the site."

ROBERT McILHARGEY,
Designer, Vancouver, B.C.

In keeping with the theme of EXPO 86, considerations for persons with disabilities were substantial. Edward de Grey, an architect with a specialty in the full integration of accessibility in building design, consulted with Expo and is the author of the requirements for persons with disabilities, part of the Expo Building Code.

"Expo is very special in terms of the disabled. It's my opinion that it's the largest integrated environment ever created in the world that is almost totally accessible…173 acres of buildings, facilities and site which are virtually barrier-free. If you take a building that's already been designed and then try to make it accessible you end up with many compromises. If you consider disabled persons with the very first thoughts on the building design you can, in fact, integrate the accessibility features so totally that they can become invisible. That was achieved at Expo."

EDWARD DE GREY,
Architect, Vancouver, B.C.

PERSPECTIVE

"The Expo Celebration, by design, is a selective taste of EXPO 86. The photographs represent a piece of the magic that could be found every day at the Exposition. The accompanying words come primarily in the form of quotations from interviews with a variety of people whose lives were touched by the Exposition.

The book is arranged in colour zones, just as the Exposition was. It takes the reader from east to west, through purple, red, blue, pink, green and yellow, stopping in between to meet people, experience wondrous performances or get involved in one of the many Special Events or Specialized Periods. The small locater map (opposite) will serve as your point of reference as you enjoy the book. Each Zone chapter begins with a highlighted version of this map, showing where you are on the 173-acre Expo site. A map, fully detailed with pavilions, buildings, facilities and attractions is on the following pages.

Look at the map, peruse the many photographs and words. Enjoy. And don't forget to wear comfortable shoes."

Producers—
The Expo Celebration,
Vancouver, B.C.

Photographer:
Peter Timmermans

LEGEND

- **SKYTRAIN**
- **MONORAIL STATION**
- **WASHROOMS**
- **INFORMATION BOOTH**
- **IBM EXPO INFO KIOSK**
- **FIRST AID AND SECURITY CENTRE**
- **FERRY**
- **SKYRIDE STATION**
- **PET KENNEL**
- **FOOD CONCESSIONS**
- **MERCHANDISE CONCESSIONS**

YELLOW ZONE □

INTERNATIONAL & PROVINCIAL
1. United States of America
2. California, Oregon, Washington
3. Republic of Korea
4. Côte d'Ivoire (Ivory Coast)
5. Cuba
51. Malaysia

CORPORATIONS & EXHIBITS
1. Great Hall of Ramses II
2. Telecom Canada
3. BCTV
4. General Motors of Canada

RIDES & ENTERTAINMENT
1. Kodak Pacific Bowl
2. Space Tower
3. Cariboo Log Chute
4. Xerox International Theatre

GREEN ZONE ▨

INTERNATIONAL & PROVINCIAL
6. Quebec
7. United Nations
8. Spain
9. Belgium
10. Italy
11. Britain
12. European Community
13. France
14. Federal Republic of Germany
15. Barbados
16. Costa Rica
17. Norway
18. Hong Kong
19. Hungary
20. Nova Scotia
21. Prince Edward Island
22. Alberta

CORPORATIONS & EXHIBITS
5. Canadian Pacific Ltd.
6. Roundhouse
7. American Express
8. Air Canada

PINK ZONE ▨

INTERNATIONAL & PROVINCIAL
23. Singapore
24. Indonesia
25. Philippines
26. Brunei Darussalam
27. Thailand
28. Union of Soviet Socialist Republics
29. Kingdom of Saudi Arabia
30. Switzerland
31. Czechoslovakia
32. South Pacific Pavilion
33. Peru
34. Sri Lanka
35. Organization of Eastern Caribbean States
36. Mexico

RIDES & ENTERTAINMENT
5. Children's Play Attraction

BLUE ZONE ■

INTERNATIONAL & PROVINCIAL
37. British Columbia

CORPORATIONS & EXHIBITS
9. Million Dollar Gold Coin

RIDES & ENTERTAINMENT
6. Expo Theatre
7. 1907 Philadelphia Toboggan Co. Carousel

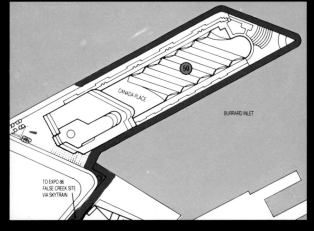

CANADA
PAVILION

RED ZONE ■

INTERNATIONAL & PROVINCIAL

- ㊳ Saskatchewan
- ㊴ Japan
- ㊵ Yugoslavia
- ㊶ Romania
- ㊷ Australia
- ㊸ Ontario
- ㊹ Kenya
- ㊺ Pakistan
- ㊻ Senegal
- ㊿ Canada (Via SkyTrain)

CORPORATIONS & EXHIBITS

- ⑩ Canadian National
- ⑪ Pavilion of Promise

RIDES & ENTERTAINMENT

- ⑧ Scream Machine
- ⑨ Looping Starship

PURPLE ZONE ■

INTERNATIONAL & PROVINCIAL

- ㊼ Yukon Territory
- ㊽ Northwest Territories
- ㊾ People's Republic of China

CORPORATIONS & EXHIBITS

- ⑫ Expo Centre
- ⑬ Folklife Festival

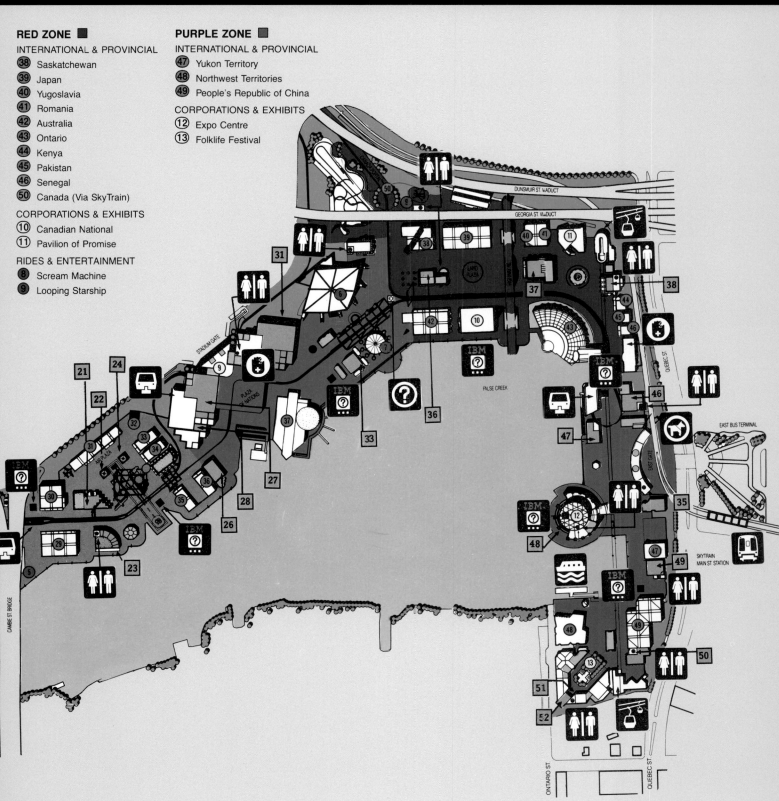

PURPLE ZONE

● *Bottom*

Expo Centre was a veteran on opening day of the Exposition, having welcomed over 600,000 guests to its theatres and displays in the year prior to May 2, 1986.

Photographer:
Rick Marotz

● *Top Right*

Night after night, vantage points staked out for hours, Expo guests watched wide-eyed as the fireworks and lasers of the Kodak International Nights of Fire lit the skies.

Photographer:
Edward M. Gifford

● *Bottom Right*

Glittering with lights and strobes, Expo Centre provided a nighttime focus for the east end of the site.

Photographer:
Edward M. Gifford

● *Top*

A Freedom to Move,
which focussed on wide-
ranging modes of
transportation displayed
Canadian Imax film
technology in Expo
Centre.

Photographer:
Brian Stablyk

● *Bottom*

The Versatron, one of
the many futuristic
vehicles shown in Expo
Centre's Design 2000.

Photographer:
Brian Stablyk

● *Top Left*

"If there are heroes of this Exposition, they are the volunteers and the people of the small towns of British Columbia who've supported us from day one.'
Jimmy Pattison,
Chairman – EXPO 86, West Vancouver, B.C.

Photographer:
Kharen Hill

● *Centre*

Design 2000, a view of the future and tie to the past as interpreted by Expo 67 designer and noted film-maker Charles Gagnon.

Photographer:
Brian Stablyk

● *Bottom*

The busiest entrance to Expo was the East Gate where, every morning, thousands coursed through the turnstiles.

Photographer:
Peter Timmermans

EXPO CENTRE BANDSTAND/
VIA RAIL

"Our Expo Centre bandstand changes from day to night. It's pretty family-oriented during the day, then at night it becomes an outside nightclub with the best view on site because you have the fireworks right there, you have the mountains and you can see the whole site lit up. It's awesome!"

Ian Warner, *Stage Manager Expo Centre Bandstand.*

Photographer:
Brian Stablyk

VIA RAIL turned a working train station into a stage for showcasing their great achievements in rail transport.

Photographer:
Doane Gregory

YUKON TERRITORY

"The sky part of our pavilion is from a Ted Harrison painting. He lives in Whitehorse. The plane is the *Queen of the Yukon*. It's the first commercially-flown aircraft in the Yukon. It's the same as Lindberg's *Spirit of St. Louis*. In fact, the *Queen of the Yukon* is the second one of these made, the *Spirit of St. Louis* was the first. It was supposed to be the other way around."
Susan Mason,
Hostess — Yukon Pavilion, Whitehorse, Yukon Territory.

Photographer:
Roger Brooks

Yukon Territory Special Day at Expo coincided with Discovery Day, August 18, in the Yukon.

Photographer:
Gunter Marx

The Rinkbinders entertained daily outside the Yukon Pavilion.

Photographer:
Norm Stelfox

● *Top*

Arms outstretched, the Inukshuk statue stood as a symbol of Northern hospitality and friendship.
Photographer:
Rick Marotz

● *Bottom*

"We call a gathering of nations like this a big games, or a gathering to have a good time. It's a *pinguarniq*."
Donald Suluk, Eskimo Point, Northwest Territories.
Photographer:
Derik Murray

●

"I found the Northwest Territories to be very impressive. I like the wide landscape and the northern lifestyle. I compared it a little bit to Scandinavia. It's open, has wilderness. That's what I like."
Josef Abderhalden, Grenchen, Switzerland.

● *Top Left*

Jimmy Pauloosie of Spence Bay, NWT, demonstrated high-kicking Arctic Sports for visitors waiting to enter the popular pavilion.

Photographer:
Darryl Snaychuk

● *Bottom Left*

High fashion from the high north. Furs from pelts to coats were on display at the Northwest Territories Pavilion.

Photographer:
Gunter Marx

● *Top Right*

Northwest Territories Pavilion host Francis Piugatiuk and his co-workers welcomed large numbers of people to view the many aspects of his home territory.

Photographer:
Heather Dean

● *Bottom Right*

The Dene Drummers from the Northwest Territories performed native rhythms in costume at Folklife.

Photographer:
Kharen Hill

21

"That's the most incredible thing about this Expo—the entertainment. It's wonderful! It's everywhere!"
Rita MacNeil, *Singer,* Cape Breton, Nova Scotia.

Photographer:
Norm Stelfox

● *Centre*

"Folklife is really different. This is the third time I've been here this week."
Joan Tisdale, Winnipeg, Manitoba.

Photographer:
Brian Stablyk

● *Bottom Left*

Foodlife, in the heart of Folklife, was always a place to find delicious aromas and tempting samples.

Photographer:
Al Harvey

● *Bottom Right*

Skillful hands, ages-old traditions and a constantly changing array of crafts were on display in Folklife.

Photographer:
Jürgen Vogt

● *Following Page*

The 'Ksan Native Dancers of Hazelton, B.C. performed *Breath of our Grandfathers,* rarely seen outside their own community.

Photographer:
Peter Timmermans

"Gates are popular forms of Chinese architecture. The symbols say *zhong hua men*, or China Gate."
Wei Ping Chao, *People's Republic Of China Pavilion.*

Photographer:
Rick Marotz

中華門

"I think one of the extraordinary things about it is that as you walk around you see the nations of the world lined up and they're all friendly. It does remind you that it's possible, doesn't it?"
Vincent Price, *Actor,* Los Angeles, California

Photographer:
Edward M. Gifford

Welcoming smiles and ancient and wondrous artifacts made the People's Republic of China Pavilion a must-see.
Photographer:
Lloyd Sutton

The Peking Pop Orchestra and Singers provided a glimpse of the modern day People's Republic of China.
Photographer:
Gunter Marx

CHINA

CEREMONIES &
THE CELEBRATED

● *Top*

Close to 70,000 guests joined royalty and officials in the May 2 opening at B.C. Place.

Photographer:
Jürgen Vogt

● *Centre*

Massed bands, colourful banners and happy smiles were the order of the day.

Photographer:
Jürgen Vogt

● *Bottom*

Royalty, dignitaries and special guests joined the crowd in the festivities.

Photographer:
Gunter Marx

Unable to enjoy much more than the ceremonies on opening day, Prime Minister Brian Mulroney brought his family to Expo in July for a leisurely visit.

Photographer:
Hans Sipma

B.C.'s government changed leaders midway through EXPO 86. Bill Bennett retired to private life and Bill Vander Zalm, here accompanied by wife Lillian at McDonald's Day, assumed the position.

Photographer:
Jürgen Vogt

● *Top*

Ontario Premier David Peterson was joined by mayors of several Ontario cities for the official Ontario Day celebrations at their amphitheatre.

Photographer:
Lloyd Sutton

● *Bottom*

Crown Prince Harald and Crown Princess Sonja of Norway presided over Norway's National Day on May 29.

Photographer:
Jürgen Vogt

"It's a tribute. Not only to the past, but to the culture of today—also to the bright role of this country in the future." **George Bush,** *Vice President—United States,* Washington, D.C.

Photographer: **Jürgen Vogt**

"When you come to a world's fair of this kind, you have a much more vivid idea of what a country can do. A country and its people. And I do think it will have a lasting influence."

Margaret Thatcher, *Prime Minister—Great Britain,* London, England.

Photographer: **Jürgen Vogt**

Famed oceanographer Jacques Cousteau brought to Expo his message of ecological peace as well as his revolutionary ship, *Alcyone.*

Photographer: **Mike Paris**

Expo Chairman Jimmy Pattison surprised all by bringing his horn to the Pavilion of Promise Special Day.

Photographer: **Gunter Marx**

Former Canadian Prime Minister Pierre Trudeau came to EXPO 86 and gave it hearty approval.

Photographer: **Alan Etkin**

Ambassador Patrick Reid, Commissioner General of EXPO 86, participated in many national and special days in the Plaza of Nations.

Photographer: **Gunter Marx**

B.C. Day, August 4, was also retiring Premier Bill Bennett's day to walk through the Expo site and be congratulated by the people of the Province.

Photographer:
Jürgen Vogt

"I didn't know what to do when I met the Prince and Princess. He went to bow...so I shook his head."
Howie Mandel,
Comedian, Los Angeles, California.

Photographer:
Jürgen Vogt

RED ZONE

● *Top*

"It seems very quiet, smooth…very efficient. It felt safe. I'd like to try it at 192 miles an hour."
Jerry Thorpe, Apache Junction, Arizona.

Photographer:
Hans Sipma

● *Bottom*

"This is a future train. There's no friction, no noise. I've enjoyed meeting all the people who've come to ride… If I could take one souvenir home, I would take a lot of souvenirs."
Minako Kuzuwa,
HSST Attendant,

Tchiba Prefecture, Japan.

Photographer:
Hans Sipma

"Canada has a wonderful potential for the future because of her rich natural resources and beautiful natural environment. This is the very first time I have ever contributed substantial amounts of funds to subsidize any exposition out of Japan. I selected this fair because of my special attachment to Vancouver and Canada."
Rioichi Sasakawa, *Honorary President— Japan Association,* Tokyo, Japan.

Photographer:
Hans Sipma

The spirit of Japan lived at EXPO 86.

Photographer:
Hans Sipma

All ages showed their heritage in performance.

Photographer:
Norm Stelfox

"Our general purpose in
the Japan Theatre is to
introduce the visitors of
Expo to real aspects of
Japanese life and
culture. We called to
everyone in Japan to
participate."
Taiichiro Ando,
*Director—P.R./Events
and Liaison, Japan
Pavilion,* Tokyo, Japan.

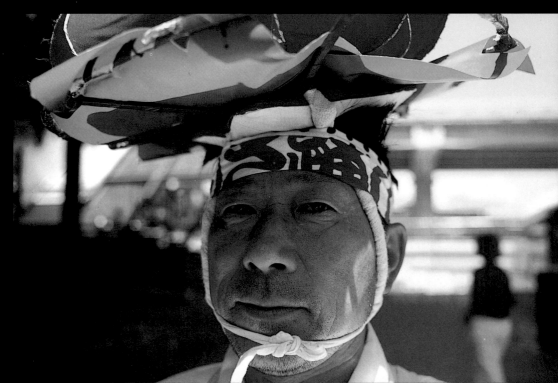

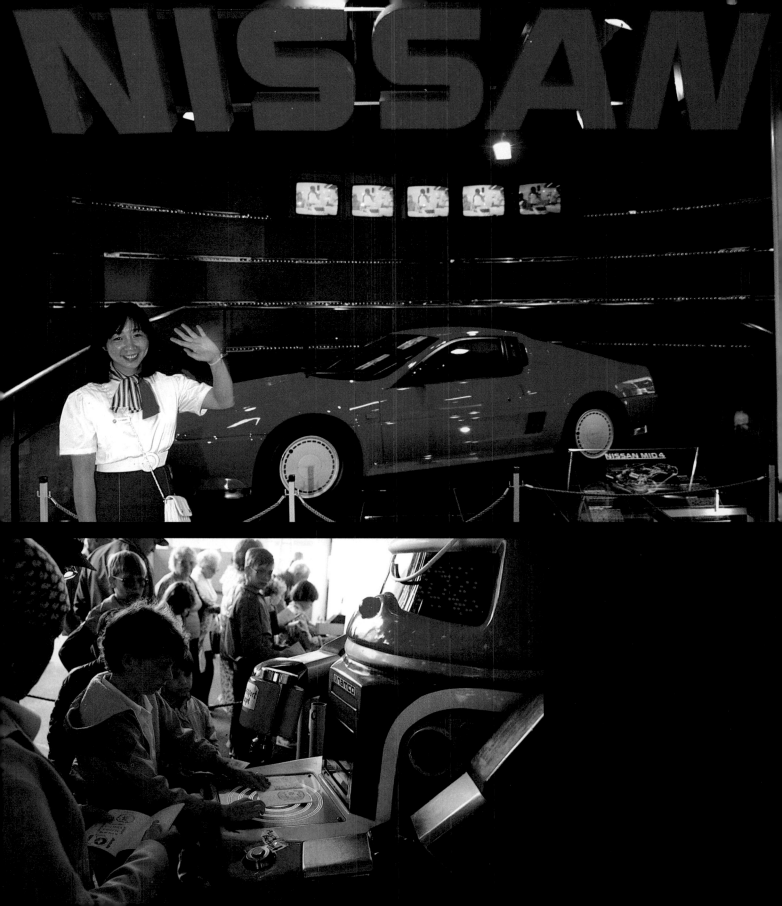

● *Top*

Hostess Shazia Cheema
of the Pakistan Pavilion
greets American visitors
Ra-Nica Monet Jackson
(left) and Angelica
Bashay.

Photographer:
Derik Murray

● *Bottom*

Art and transport were
the focus for Senegal's
pavilion at EXPO 86.

Photographer:
John Kenny

● *Top*

Part of a world in motion, the country of Yugoslavia welcomed streams of visitors through its pavilion during the fair.

Photographer:
Jürgen Vogt

● *Bottom*

Visitors to Romania's Pavilion experienced everything from miracles in music to triumphs in modern transportation.

Photographer:
Stuart N. Dee

EXIT →

"It was our last night at Expo, so we went to the Trillium Restaurant in the Ontario Pavilion. We had a terrific dinner, but it was especially good when you consider we also saw a great show in

their amphitheatre and then had the best view of the fireworks."
Maureen Jones,
Whitevale, Ontario.

Photographer:
Greg Athans

A view to the west from the Trillium Restaurant in the Ontario Pavilion.

Photographer:
Jürgen Vogt

"The tunnel before the film was excellent. You started out walking through Niagara Falls and it was almost as if you were walking through them! I've never been there before so it was fantastic."
Bill Adair,
Prince George, B.C.

Photographer:
Norm Stelfox

Photographer:
Lloyd Sutton

SASKATCHEWAN

sculptor Bill Lishman, was the centrepiece of the Land Plaza.

Photographer:
Albert Normandin

But every one of them means something to the place it came from. There's a bit of the past and a bit of the future here. The sculpture in the middle ties it together."
Terry DeSantos,
Sacramento, California.

"The vehicles were right there, you could put your hands on them. You feel like you're on the streets...and it gives you more than just an exhibit feeling. It's a presence."
Tannis Hopkins,
Vancouver, B.C.

● *Top Left*

Photographer:
William P. McElligott

● *Bottom Left*

Photographer:
Janis A. Kraulis

● *Top Right*

Photographer:
Alan Etkin

● *Bottom Centre*

Photographer:
Kharen Hill

● *Bottom Right*

"I even met a man who used to drive one of these trucks and another man, about 60, who got a ride home in one when he was a boy and hadn't seen one since."
'Ace' McKay Smith,
Hostess—Labatt's Stream-liner, with **Donald Keele,** Vancouver, B.C.

Photographer:
Derik Murray

● *Facing Page*

Following their victory at Rescue 86, part of the Expo Specialized Period on Search and Rescue, the Australian team showed off another great Aussie sea winner, *Australia II*.

Photographer:
Jürgen Vogt

●*Top*

"We saw a lot of things on them winning the America's Cup. At least three times they mentioned it! But, what the heck, I don't blame them at all."
Shirley Martin,
St. Albert, Alberta.

Photographer:
Gunter Marx

●*Bottom Left*

Veteran crowd-pleaser Rolf Harris tied his kangaroo down long enough to partake in Australia National Day, June 18. (Or "eye-deenth" if you wish.)

Photographer:
Gunter Marx

●*Bottom Right*

"We have an Expo in 1988 in Australia. I hope you will come. We'd like to see how you dance, how you sing…"
John Ralkurru,
Aborigine Performer.
Arnhemland, Northern Territory, Australia.

Photographer:
Derik Murray

● *Top Left*

Commissioner David
Mainse, host of the
popular TV show 100
Huntley Street, broadcasts
from the Pavilion of
Promise.

Photographer:
Hans Sipma

● *Top Right*

"You can come away
immediately with
something here. Here
you can walk away with
God in your life."
Robert Zamida, *Host—
Pavilion of Promise,*
Toronto, Ontario.

Photographer:
Michael Morissette

● *Bottom Left*

"I love meeting the
people, love talking to
them and being able to
share about my faith in
Jesus Christ.
The theme of our
pavilion is God's desire
to communicate with
man and we believe his
desire comes through
Jesus Christ."

Ann Crocker, *Hostess—
Pavilion of Promise,*
Vancouver, B.C.

Photographer:
Gunter Marx

● *Bottom Right*

June 7 was the Special
Day for the Pavilion of
Promise, a day more
than worthy of a parade.

Photographer:
Gunter Marx

● *Top Left*

Highlighting Kenya
National Day, June 9,
the Bomas Harambee
Dancers from Nairobi.

Photographer:
Albert Normandin

● *Top Right*

The Bomas performed
in the Plaza of Nations
showing Expo guests
the traditional costumes,
instruments and dance
movements of their
native tribe.

Photographer:
Gunter Marx

● *Bottom Left*

A warm welcome was
always to be found at
the Kenya Pavilion.

Photographer:
Perry Zavitz

● *Bottom Right*

"I was actually born in
Kenya. On the coast of
East Africa, it's like
Hawaii."
Jill Edgar,
Vancouver, B.C.

Photographer:
Perry Zavitz

● *Top*

Never too old, never too young to enjoy UFO-H2O.

Photographer:
Stuart N. Dee

● *Facing Page*

"Well, I always think 'kid'—even when I'm thinking for adults. Because I always deal with the child inside, under the skin. That's the common denominator. It's the kid in everybody. Almost everything I do has a toy-like quality, you might say, which is calculated to disarm and charm to reach the something way-down inside...the nostalgia, the childhood. Adults participate through the children. I can sit and watch the kids here but I don't have to get wet myself. It's nice if you do..."

John Martin Gilbert, *Creator—UFO-H2O,* West Vancouver, B.C.

Photographer:
Alex Waterhouse-Hayward

● *Bottom*

"It looks like a UFO about to take off for another planet and these are creatures from this planet and it's squirting water to say good-bye on something that looks like a mushroom."
Christine Tazares, *age* 12, Los Angeles, California.

Photographer:
Stuart N. Dee

● *Facing Page*

"Our aim is to get people a little more interested in the physics of motion because, at CN, we're into railways, communications. We move things and we also move facts. Motion is the theme, but it's also a lot of fun."
Randy Jordan,
Host—CN Pavilion.
Burnaby, B.C.

Photographer:
Gunter Marx

● *Top*

CN hosts circled their pavilion with 'roller blades', a combination of ice skates and roller skates.

Photographer:
Lloyd Sutton

● *Bottom*

CN used coloured symbols to illustrate the forms of motion. The blue bar for uniform motion, the red semi-circle for circular motion, the yellow slanted bar for accelerating motion and the green 'S' for oscillatory motion.

Photographer:
Jürgen Vogt

● *Top Right*

"Oh, yes, everyone thinks I was here to perform at Expo Theatre on Australia Day...but the truth is, I came for the Scream Machine. You won't tell anyone, will you? I went on it three times!"
Peter Allen, *Singer*, New York, New York.

Photographer:
Edward M. Gifford

● *Left*

"When they get on the ride, I take their parcels. Then the lap bar comes down over their legs and shoulders. We check them to make sure they're snug and then off they go. When they're upside down, they feel weightlessness.

Sometimes they go around twice, sometimes it's three times. It depends on how much they weigh."
Clint Marquette, *Looping Starship Attendant*, North Vancouver, B.C.

Photographer:
Derik Murray

● *Bottom Right*

"AAAAOOOOEEEE!!!"
Rob Munro, Toronto, Ontario; **Colin Scott**, Vancouver, B.C.

Photographer:
Derik Murray

● *Facing Page*

"I believe that I married the Scream Machine..."
Coral Brown (Mrs. Vincent Price), *Actress*, Los Angeles, California.

Photographer:
Edward M. Gifford

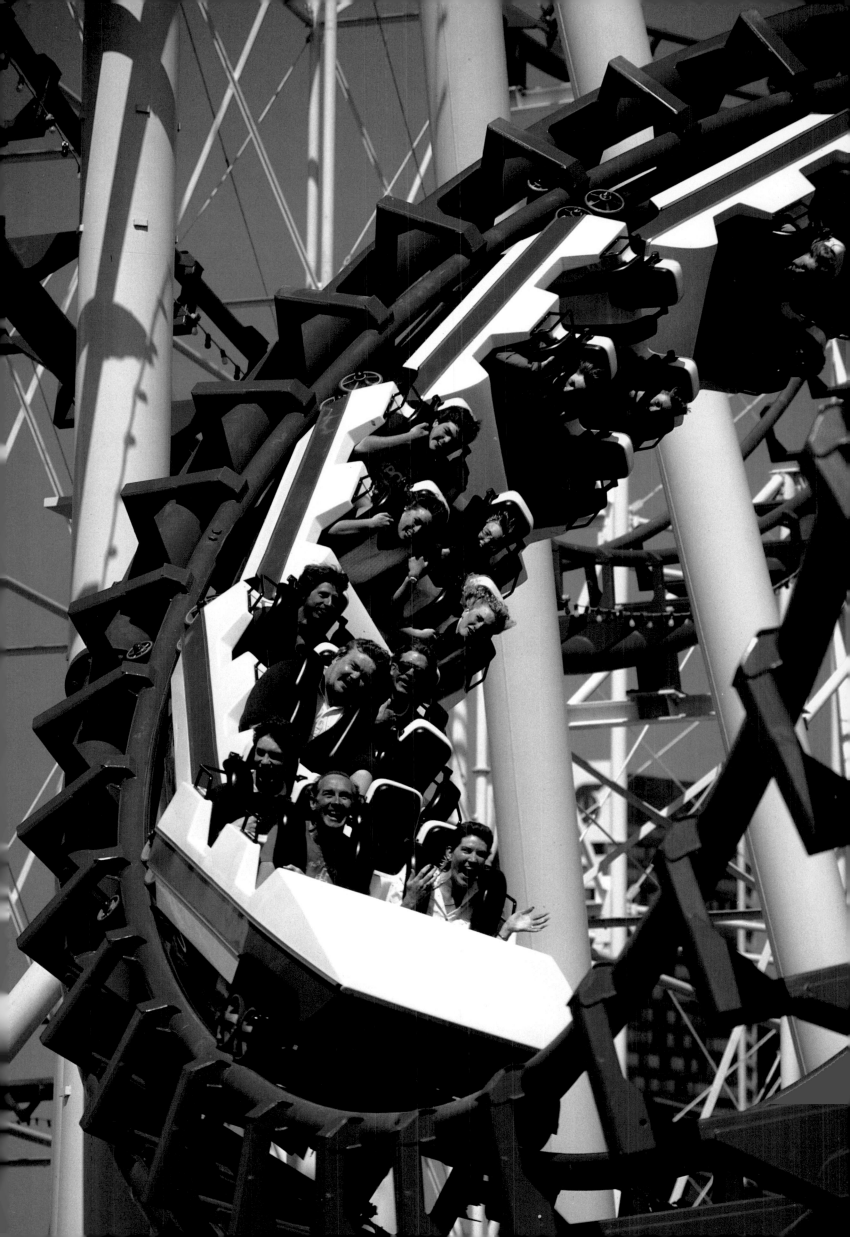

● *Top Left*

Bigfoot meets Big Puck
at the Canada Portal.

Photographer:
Stuart N. Dee

● *Top Right*

The almost-famous
Hamburger Hockey
League at the very
famous, world's largest
hockey stick.

Photographer:
Al Harvey

● *Bottom Left*

Two more reasons for
one guest visiting the
Red Zone.

Photographer:
John Kenny

● *Bottom Right*

Canada Portal: Gateway
to the wonders of the
Canada Pavilion.

Photographer:
Perry Zavitz

CANADA PAVILION

● *Bottom Right*

"The Canada Pavilion is perhaps the most photographed structure next to the refurbished Statue of Liberty. I had the opportunity of sailing into the cruise ship facility with Vice President George Bush and Mrs. Bush and he was absolutely awestruck by the beauty and the magnificence of it."
Don Mazankowski, *Deputy Prime Minister/ Minister Responsible—* EXPO 86, Ottawa, Ontario.

Photographer: **Janis Kraulis**

● *Previous Pages*

The Canada Pavilion created a lasting impact on its host city by changing the skyline forever.

Photographer:
Peter Timmermans

● *Top Left*

Ready for an electrifying experience at the entrance to the Canada Pavilion.

Photographer:
Jürgen Vogt

● *Top Centre*

Rail transport, the focus of Rebecca Burke's perpetual motion machine on display in the Great Hall under the sails.

Photographer:
Stuart N. Dee

● *Top Right*

Celebrating their golden anniversary, CBC broadcast daily from Canada Pavilion with an incredible panorama as a backdrop. Pictured clockwise, hosts of Newscentre—Cecilia Walters, Bill Good Jr., Phil Reimer, and J. Paul McConnell.

Photographer:
Doane Gregory

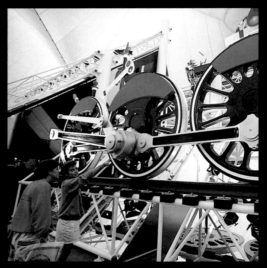

● *Bottom Left*

"We wanted to say how, in a country the size of Canada, the transportation and communication systems are inextricably linked. The Vidiwall makes it an exciting story."
Dick Lott, *Coordinator— Design Development, Canada Pavilion,*

● *Bottom Centre*

"I love the Imax in 3-D. I would love to make a 3-D movie. Can you imagine a thriller in 3-D? I could get the bullets to fly right to you."
George Cosmatos, *Director—Rambo: First Blood Part 2,* Victoria, B.C.

● *Bottom Right*

Shorelines, an active collection of works of art and technology depicting the varied and important life on Canada's coasts.

Photographer:
Jürgen Vogt

● *Facing Page*

"I like to play with things, see what they do with light and colour. And then there's the music."
Michel Lemieux.
Performance Artist, Montreal, Quebec.

Photographer:
Jürgen Vogt

● *Facing Page*

The Hystar, an aerodome saucer, floats high above the crowds in the Great Hall of the Canada Pavilion. "Logging, petroleum, agriculture, construction, telecommunications, tourism and recreation are only a few of the industries that will benefit from Hystar. It has unlimited application in air transport, especially where access rather than speed is the prime consideration."
George Ninkovich, *President—Hystar Aerospace Development Corporation,* Vancouver, B.C.

Photographer:
Brian Stablyk

● *Top*

Kwak_utl artist Simon Dick's noble Thunderbird sculpture presided over countless performances in the outdoor amphitheatre.

Photographer:
Norm Stelfox

● *Bottom Left*

Vancouver's Extraordinary Clown Band, starring Henry Davis, Emry Laird and Lotte Dog.

Photographer:
Jürgen Vogt

● *Bottom Right*

"It's so hard to come up with the definitive statement of what I do because every time I do it it's different from the time before!"
Al Simmons, *Performer,* Anola, Manitoba.

Photographer:
Gunter Marx

BLUE ZONE

BRITISH
COLUMBIA
PAVILION

● *Top*

Authentic totem poles
stood sentry along
the walkway leading
to the Discovery portion
of the BC Pavilion. The
miniature forest was a
microcosm of B.C.

Photographer:
Lloyd Sutton

● *Top Left*

The BC Pavilion was
divided, also, with
Discovery at water's
edge and Challenge at
the opposite side of the
Plaza of Nations.

Photographer.
Peter Timmermans

● *Bottom Left*

Inside innovative
'Trees of Discovery,'
audio-visuals by
Vancouver's Creative
House introduced
millions of visitors
to the advances and
successes of BC
technology.

Photographer:
Barry Brooks

● *Bottom Right*

"It's as if the Exposition
happened to go through
part of the existing city.
It's busy, it's bustling,
it's an urban square."
Clive Grout, *Architect,*
Waisman Dewar Grout
Carter, Vancouver, B.C.

Photographer:
Rick Marotz

Dockside at the East Wharf, the highest of marine technology was exemplified by the BC designed and built *Atlantis II* submarine.

Photographer:
Stephe Tate

The Boom Boat Ballet was a whimsical choreography of maritime workhorses. "It was Al Dickey at Rivtow's idea and he approached the BC Pavilion. It was great fun, they were great learners and they were cute! Next time I want to do it with helicopters!"
Viktoria Langton.
Choreographer,
Vancouver, B.C.

Photographer:
Norm Stelfox

In the Challenge Pavilion, *Our British Columbia*, a film featuring British Columbians playing themselves. Directed by Richard Jeffries, it featured the three-screen Tri-Max format. "I thought *Our British Columbia* was stunning. The wide screen made you feel like you were there...a part of it."
Marjorie Collins,
Richmond B.C.

Photographer
Brian Stablyk

Cinematographer:
Bruce Ingram (1945–1986)

BC actress Fairuza Balk met a friendly alien named Zargon in *Discovery*, a film in the Discovery Pavilion. "I just couldn't resist the opportunity to create a show using the finest BC talent, the finest BC crew, the incredible new Showscan film technology and the finest location in the world—BC."
Rob Turner,
Director—Discovery,
President—Circle Productions,
Vancouver, B.C.

Photographer:
Chris Helcermanas Benge

The 1907 Philadelphia
Toboggan Company
Carousel.
"Now this is the kind
of ride I like. It has all
the thrills I need!"
Grace Jacobsen, Fort
Worth, Texas.

Photographer:
Janis Kraulis

Expo through the eyes
(monitor?) of the official
mascot ambassador of
EXPO 86, Expo Ernie.

Photographer:
Edward M. Gifford

● *Top*

The ever-present Expo Ernie attracted crowds wherever he went, always making friends.

Photographer:
Jürgen Vogt

● *Bottom Left*

Bernie Casavant, chef at the elegant Canadian Club, prepared some of the most elaborate food on site.

Photographer:
Hans Sipma

● *Bottom Centre*

"I am, myself, a human mobile pavilion. People come and talk to me and they say, 'You're a great ambassador.' Some of them have never seen the flag pin of their country so they get quite excited when they see it. They call me the king of pins!"
Haje Protais,
Expo Volunteer,
Vancouver, B.C.

Photographer:
Joseph Lederer

● *Bottom Right*

Each and every night at 10:30, Glen Priest and co-workers Misha Tarasoff and Pamela Loughton electrified the nighttime sky with the Kodak International Nights of Fire from a barge in False Creek.

Photographer:
Alex Waterhouse-Hayward

"It made sense for Kodak to sponsor the International Nights of Fire. We're into spectacular pictures and they don't come much better than this. The colours, the shapes and the music make it much more than just a fireworks show. I can't count the number of times I've sat and watched them with the family. It just gets better and better.
"I think it's probably the best way possible to end a day in Expo. You don't have to do anything. Find a comfortable place to watch. Then you just sit back and enjoy."
Peter Little,
Sales Manager,
Professional and
Finishing Markets,
(Western Canada),
Kodak Canada Inc.,
North Vancouver, B.C.
Photographer:
Gunter Marx

● *Preceding Pages*

One of the most
striking pieces of
architecture on the
Expo s███, ███he Plaza
of Nations came alive
after dark.

Photographer:
Rick Marotz

● *Facing Page*

"If there was any trend
to be learned from the
last of the BC Style
fashion presentations
at Expo…it was that
fashion today runs the
gamut from classic
to avant garde, from
practical to audacious,
and the contingent of

BC talent showed
it all."
Virginia Leeming,
Fash██ Reporter, The
Vancouver Sun,
Vancouver, B.C.

Photographer:
Kharen Hill

● *Top Left*

Renowned throughout
the world for playing
unique music in unique
locales, flautist Paul
Horn took part in
BC Celebration as well.
BC Celebration was the
dream of composer
Robbie King.

Photographer:
Gunter Marx

● *Top Right*

On█ o█ BC's busiest
singers █ane Mortifee
was a highlight of the
big BC Celebration
show on the eve of
BC Day.

Photographer:
Gunter Marx

● *Bottom Left*

Th█ █l█ of Nations
serve█ ███host to many
dance and musical
group█ █ncluding the
Karry Krich Kidco
Dance Company of
Victoria.

Photographer:
Gunter Marx

● *Bottom Right*

Free, open-air concerts
on the Plaza of Nations
stage included the very
best in professional
talent—such as Doug
and the Slugs—as well
as amateur performers.

Photographer:
Gunter Marx

●

A striking structure with a profound purpose, the Plaza of Nations was more than simply a stage, some seats and an impressive roof line. it was the place where the world met.

● *Preceding Pages*

The Plaza of Nations was the centre of many days, such as BC Day. A massive birthday cake, divided amongst the thousands of guests, performances by a variety of BC artists and much ceremony was a day in the life of the gathering place.

Photographer:
Jürgen Vogt

● *Facing Page*

Eagerly anticipating an Expo debut, young performers at the BC Bandshell are keeping a keen eye open for talent scouts.

Photographer:
Albert Normandin

● *Top Left*

"I see the Hollywood image of the Indian everywhere and through my performances I'm just trying to show the pride of today and the pride of tomorrow. I'm not a politician, I'm an entertainer. I just want to see a greater understanding of Native People amongst all people."
Ernie Philips,
Entertainer, Shuswap Band, Haney, B.C.
Photographer:
Gunter Marx

● *Top Right*

The Utah Valley Stars, just some of the 65,000 performers who appeared at Expo as part of the Amateur and Heritage Program.

Photographer:
Stuart N. Dee

● *Bottom Left*

The strong sense of national pride knew no bounds of age when Expo celebrated a National Day.

Photographer:
Larry Goldstein

● *Bottom Right*

At McDonald's Corporate Day, wheel-chair athlete Rick Hansen connected with the Plaza of Nations by phone, where Vice President Ron Marcoux presented him with the promise of a minimum quarter-million-dollar contribution to the Man in Motion World Tour.

Photographer:
Jürgen Vogt

● *Top*

" There's a real turnover all the time. And you have a great mix of people. Not only do you have Canadians, you have Americans, you have Europeans...it's a continuous turnover." **Billy Newton Davis,** *Singer,* Toronto, Ontario.

Photographer:
Brian Stablyk

● *Bottom Left*

England's Ra Ra Zoo at The Flying Club, which also hosted the famed Second City comedy troupe.

Photographer:
Albert Normandin

● *Bottom Right*

"It's a fabulous room to play. The exposure is good for everybody. I think it changes your profile in the city, the fact that you've played there. Out of this city, probably 10 to 15 percent of the bands that are in the city played 86 Street and the rest haven't, so getting lucky enough to play in there was terrific." **Hank Leonhardt,** *Lead Singer—The Toasters,* Vancouver, B.C.

Photographer:
Dee Lippingwell

LABATT'S
EXPO THEATRE

● *Top*

Labatt's Legends of Rock 'n' Roll, held on a succession of Sundays, brought the true cornerstones of American popular music, such as Roy Orbison to Expo.

Photographer:
Glen Erikson

● *Centre*

Memories rekindled, musical roots rediscovered, the Legends series at Expo Theater brought together audiences old and young in a celebration of a North American art form—rock and roll.

Photographer:
Glen Erikson

● *Upper Centre*

Kicking off the Legends series, Carl Perkins played music from the class of '55, a pivotal point in rock and roll that included the early roots of Elvis Presley's career.

Photographer:
Glen Erikson

● *Bottom Left*

"You talk to people like Ray Charles. Rock and roll was responsible for ending the racial problem in America. There was a lot to say for the international language of music acting as a catalyst to bring people together."
Red Robinson,
Producer/Host, Labatt's Legends of Rock 'n' Roll,
Vancouver, B.C.

Photographer:
Albert Normandin

● *Lower Centre*

Don and Phil Everly, music history personified and a highlight of the Legends of Rock 'n' Roll series.

Photographer:
Glen Erikson

● *Previous Page*

Dashing, romantic, and completely sold out months in advance, Mikhail Baryshnikov and Company stunned audiences with their dance prowess. They were stunning not only in performance, but as pictured here, in rehearsal as well.

Photographer:
David Cooper

● *Top Left*

Expo Theatre became the glitterdome for a week while Liberace brought his Las Vegas act out of the US for the very first time.

Photographer:
Jürgen Vogt

● *Top Centre*

Perennial Vancouver favourite Mitzi Gaynor brought her high-stepping show to Expo Theatre. Vancouver is almost a second home to Gaynor and as a result, local audiences witness each year's new shows before the rest of the world.

Photographer:
Albert Normandin

● *Top Right*

Québec en Fête hosted star Francophone entertainers in a live broadcast event.
"It's St. Jean Baptiste Day and we're going to party."
Rene Simard, *Singer,*
Montreal, Quebec.

Photographer:
Gunter Marx

● *Bottom Left*

The du Maurier International Jazz Festival brought to Expo the very finest in jazz talent from around the world, including American trumpet superstar, Wynton Marsalis.

Photographer:
Jürgen Vogt

● *Bottom Centre*

Edmonton's k. d. lang brought her own inimitable style and repertoire to Expo Theatre, celebrating the very best in original Canadian music.

Photographer:
Dee Lippingwell

● *Bottom Right*

"People have impressions of Canada other than the clichés of toques and beer. We're seen as an independent nation, one that has a voice in the world."
Bruce Cockburn,
Singer,
Toronto, Ontario.

Photographer:
Dee Lippingwell

SPECIALIZED PERIODS/
SPECIAL EVENTS

"The theme of this exposition lent itself to a breakdown of the whole vista of what might be accomplished in terms of transportation and communication into components. It's just too large and complex to be developed into one particular package. "We would not have had the representation we do have had we not extended the theme of the exposition, both in the physical and developmental sense, beyond the actual physical confines of the exposition."
Patrick Reid,
Ambassador/Commissioner General — EXPO 86.
Vancouver, B.C.

Canadian precision
military aerobatic
team, The Snowbirds,
delighted guests with
numerous appearances
at Expo.

Photographer:
Brian Stablyk

The British Airways
Concorde flew over the
Expo site on Britain
National Day and was
one of the highlights of
the Specialized Period
on Aviation.

Photographer:
Stephe Tate

Competitors in the
Expo Invitational
International Skydiving
Competition jumped
from 3000 feet to land
on a two-inch disc.

Photographer:
Norm Stelfox

In celebration of the
50th anniversary of the
DC-3, *Odyssey* 86 carried
the Expo message
around the world.

Photographer:
Hans Sipma

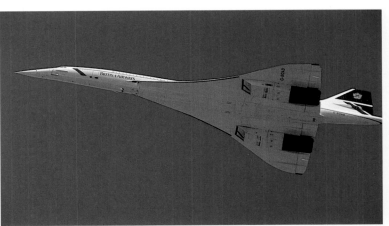

● *Top Left*

● *Bottom Left*

● *Top Right*

● *Bottom Right*

Autorodeo Vaz, spectacular stunts by Russian drivers, thrilled audiences at the Kodak Pacific Bowl during the Specialized Period on Automobiles.

Photographer:
Hans Sipma

Alternative Fuel and Power Systems for Transportation brought world-class innovations such as the Solarbolid Biel 2 from Switzerland.

Photographer:
Peter Timmermans

The Innovative Vehicle Design Competition, part of the Automotive Specialized Period, was won by the University of British Columbia.

Photographer:
Gunter Marx

"It just seemed so logical with an exposition theme of transportation and communications that our culture acknowledge the canoe. So the Glwa Expedition brought us 500 kilometres from Bella Bella to Expo." **Frank Brown,** *Glwa Organizer,* Waglisla, B.C.

Photographer:
Gunter Marx

Captain Jacques Cousteau's highly innovative Turbosail vessel, the *Alcyone*, gave Expo guests a taste of truly remarkable marine technology.

Photographer:
Albert Chin

The 100-metre *Nippon Maru* Tall Ship joined other ships of the world, part of the Specialized Period on Marine Commerce.

Photographer:
Rick Marotz

● *Top*

"We've got a really international competition here. Skateboarders from all over the world."
Monty Little,
Organizer—Transworld Skateboard Championships, Vancouver, B.C.

Photographer:
Thomas Bruckbauer

● *Bottom Left*

As part of the Specialized Period on Transportation for Recreation, skateboarders performed at several locations both on and off the Expo site.

Photographer:
Norm Stelfox

● *Bottom* Centre

Diane Desiderio of Ocean Beach, California was one of the international contingent here to compete.

Photographer:
Jürgen Vogt

● *Bottom Right*

Vancouver lifeguard Stan Shibler took part in the Specialized Period on Search and Rescue by competing in Rescue 86.

Photographer:
Larry Goldstein

● *Top*

"It's my hope that Gift Of Wings, Canada's first coast to coast ultralight flight, will raise awareness of the situation of the spinal cord injured in Canada and worldwide."
Carl Hiebert,
Paraplegic Pilot,
Kitchener, Ontario.

Photographer:
Jürgen Vogt

● *Centre*

The Hong Kong Dragon Boat Festival– International Races 1986 brought competitors from all over the world in a spirit of friendly challenge.

Photographer:
Albert Chin

● *Bottom*

Ten years after the annual Dragon Boat Festival began in Hong Kong, the ancient races are now a popular international sporting event.

Photographer:
Albert Chin

STEAMEXPO was a chance for everyone to get involved in the thrill of the rails.

Photographer:
Jürgen Vogt

Photographer:
Jürgen Vogt

The Specialized Period on Urban Transit brought experts from around the world. B.C. was particularly proud of its newly installed Advanced Light Rail Transport (ALRT) or Skytrain.

Photographer:
Rick Marotz

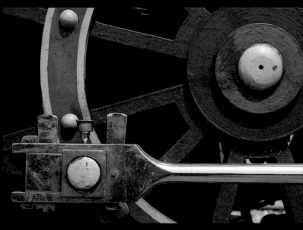

Grand Parade of Steam
during STEAMEXPO.

Photographer:
Jürgen Vogt

TWO-SPOT

● *Top Left*

Communications and
Mobility for Elderly and
Disabled People brought
able-bodied and disabled
together.

Photographer:
Gunter Marx

● *Top Right*

"It's believing in a
dream. Knowing that as
I wheel around the
world in the Man In
Motion Tour I can help
raise awareness of the
potential of the
disabled."
Rick Hansen,
*Wheelchair Athlete — Man
In Motion World Tour,*
Vancouver, B.C.

Photographer:
Gordon Schuck

● *Bottom Left*

The waters of False
Creek were alive with
the sights and sounds of
the Formula One Power
Boat Races, part of the
Specialized Period on
Transportation for
Recreation.

Photographer:
Tim Harvey

● *Bottom Right*

Polar Transportation
and Communications,
the first of the
Specialized Periods,
hosted an impressive
flypast of Arctic and
bush aircraft.

Photographer:
Hans Sipma

● *Top*

From July 20 to 25, Expo held its Specialized Period on Communications and Mobility for Elderly and Disabled People.

Photographer:
Kharen Hill

● *Centre Left*

The Specialized Period on Human-Powered Transportation brought many streamlined and innovative vehicles, all making the most of human potential for mobility.

Photographer:
Gunter Marx

● *Top Right*

The Dal Richards Big Band had seniors swinging at the Plaza of Nations on Seniors' Showcase Day.

Photographer:
Al Harvey

● *Bottom Left*

June 1 was International Children's Day at Expo. Spritely Danny Kaye, Ambassador-at-Large for the UN Children's Fund, showed age is just a state of mind.

Photographer:
Gunter Marx

● *Bottom Right*

All the way from 100 Mile House, the *Ride of a Lifetime* comes to an end at Expo.

Photographer:
Gunter Marx

PINK ZONE

● *Bottom*

"The intermingling of ancient traditions and cultures of the Malay Archipelago, China and India with the hustle and bustle of a modern city forms the unique charm of Singapore."
Dr. Tony Tan,
Minister of Education,
Singapore.

Photographer:
Jürgen Vogt

● *Top Right*

Goods of every size, shape and colour could be found in the Indonesian market display.

Photographer:
Albert Normandin

● *Centre Right*

"The architecture of the Singapore Pavilion is basically a Chinese house with a certain amount of Malay motifs and a lot of Western influence."
Liang-Hye Lee,
*Assistant Manager—
Singapore Pavilion*,
Singapore.

Photographer:
Norm Stelfox

● *Bottom Right*

"Brunei Darussalam is on the island of Borneo's northwest coast. Oil and natural gas make us one of the most prosperous nations in the world."
Mike Wong, *Host—
Brunei Darussalam
Pavilion*, Brunei
Darussalam.

Photographer:
John Kenny

● *Facing Page*

The brightly coloured arches or *pandals* in the Sri Lanka Pavilion attracted many interesting Expo guests. At Expo, as at home, the arches indicate a festive occasion.

Photographer:
Ric Kokotovich

● *Top*

The Tower Hall Dance Ensemble performed in traditional costume on Sri Lanka Day, July 24.

Photographer:
Gunter Marx

● *Centre*

Mexico's Inca Warrior was kept busy posing when not performing the traditional 'Dance of Quetzalcoatl', the dance of the plumed serpent.

Photographer:
Perry Zavitz

● *Bottom*

Featured in the Mexico Pavilion was a fragment of the Madrid Codex. Of Mayan origin, the codex is a ritualistic almanac with forecasts for each day.

Photographer:
Simon Scott

● *Top*

"These masks are actually stools, orator stools from the Highlands of New Guinea. During the Yam Festival, the Orator sits on the seat and speaks of the harvest and of next year's harvest or whatever business the tribe has for the next year."
Robert Helu, *Host— South Pacific Pavilion*, Nukualofa, Tonga.

Photographer:
Darryl Snaychuk

● *Bottom Right*

All aspects of South Pacific's beauty were shown to the fullest at EXPO 86.

Photographer:
Jürgen Vogt

● *Top*

Ceremony, tradition and necessity joined hands as the summer weather turned in as fine a performance as the people of the Philippines.

Photographer:
Albert Normandin

● *Bottom*

Intricate native costumes and colourful customs made the Philippines National Day, June 12, a memorable event.

Photographer:
Patrick Morrow

SWITZERLAND

● *Top*

"We were all discovered in the first three voyages of Christopher Columbus and we were all colonized by the British. St. Lucia and Dominica have a lot of French dominance, mainly because they're so close to the French islands."

"If you know the history, St. Lucia's been fought over so many times by the French and British, they call her the 'Helen of the West' after Helen of Troy."
Jeannette Cadet,
Assistant Manager—
O.E.C.S. Pavilion,
St. Vincent and The Grenadines.

Photographer:
Peter Timmermans

● *Bottom*

From Antigua/Barbuda, the members of The Harmonites played steel band melodies for OECS Day crowds.

Photographer:
Rick Marotz

● *Top Left*

"We're saying thank you for helping us. We're here to help you, too."
Enrique Cedron Morales, *Manager—Peru Pavilion*, Lima, Peru.

Photographer:
Kharen Hill

● *Top Right*

Photographer:
Jürgen Vogt

● *Centre*

The well-dressed *Paso Peruano*—Peruvian walking horse—wears a halter, bridle and *tapa ojos* (blinder) made of plaited goat hide and decorated with carved silver.

Photographer:
Norm Stelfox

● *Bottom*

The most important pieces from the Peru Gold Museum—some 265 in all—showcased the art, engineering and culture of the Inca Empire.

Photographer:
Simon Scott

● *Top*

Massive murals on the exterior of the Saudi Arabia Pavilion depicted desert scenes and the ancient cities of Najran and Alwajh.

Photographer:
Perry Zavitz

● *Centre*

"We only get the impression that Saudi Arabia is oil. That's what they're known for. But I did see more than that. It's a kingdom, you know."
Martha Tallis,
Toronto, Ontario.

Photographer:
Hans Sipma

● *Bottom Left*

Constantly posing for photos, staff at the Saudi Arabia Pavilion were proud of their native costumes.

Photographer:
John Kenny

THAILAND

● *Top*

The ASEAN Plaza at Expo was sponsored by the Association of Southeast Asian Nations. Here the Philippines, Brunei, Thailand, Indonesia, Singapore and Malaysia presented many cultural events—which some

Expo visitors did more than simply enjoy!

Photographer:
Gunter Marx

● *Bottom Left*

Thailand celebrated its National Day July 22.

Photographer:
John Kenny

● *Bottom Right*

Thotsakan, the Demon King of Lonka, has the power to transform himself into a colossal superbeing with 10 heads and 20 arms. This statue is an exact replica of the one that guards the Royal Chapel in Bangkok.

Photographer:
Gunter Marx

● *Top Left*

Known for innovative and exciting pavilions at previous expositions, Czechoslovakia outdid themselves at EXPO 86.

Photographer:
Michael Morissette

● *Top Right*

The Domenik group from Czechoslovakia celebrated victory after a staged duel with dancing. Their staged fights were, at times, almost too realistic.

Photographer:
Norm Stelfox

● *Bottom*

"We were involved in many aspects of Expo. We had the festival of Czechoslovakian crystal glass as a tribute. We took part in the Specialized Periods. In urban transit, we showed our trams. We took part in railway transport. We brought over our world aerobatic champion who took part in the Canada Open Championship.
"We were very glad to do all these things. It also gave us a good platform for the future."
Ladislav Kopecky,
Director of Public Relations—Czechoslovakia Pavilion, Prague, Czechoslovakia.

Photographer:
Doane Gregory

● *Top*

Large and colourful, the Pajeng of Bali shaded the entrance of the Indonesia Pavilion.

Photographer:
Peter Timmermans

● *Bottom*

Bappenas, a brain trust within the government of Indonesia, has staged the growth of the country in five-year plans called *Repelitas*. Now in their fourth Repelita, they expect to achieve their potential by the end of the sixth plan.

Photographer:
Edward M. Gifford

● *Top*

For obvious reasons, the rickshaw outside the Indonesia Pavilion rated high on the Exposition's most-photographed list.

Photographer:
Ric Kokotovich

● *Bottom*

Indonesia brought one of their naval training ships, the *Dewa Ruci*, to Expo for their National Day, August 20.

Photographer:
Jürgen Vogt

UNION OF SOVIET SOCIALIST REPUBLICS

● *Top*

Celebrating 25 years of manned space flight, the USSR themed its pavilion "Transport and Communication for Peace and Cooperation."

Photographer:
Edward M. Gifford

● *Bottom Left*

The Soyuz-Salyut-Progress orbital complex was used for cosmonaut training prior to its installation at Expo. The Salyut 7, launched in 1982 from a complex much like this, flew in near-earth orbit over Canada more than a dozen times during the Exposition.

Photographer:
Jürgen Vogt

● *Bottom Right*

The Big Children's Chorus of Moscow Radio and Television joined many other children's choirs June 1 to celebrate Children's Day at Expo.

Photographer:
Gunter Marx

"When you see the transportation and communication advances that are on display, you really get a sense that the world is a community. It does bring people closer together."

Alan Bergman, *Composer*, Los Angeles, California.

Photographer: **Al Harvey**

An eight-metre-high sculpture of Yuri Gagarin, the first man in space, welcomed Expo guests to the entrance of the USSR Pavilion.

Photographer: **Gunter Marx**

Nothing could discourage the daily line-ups at the USSR Pavilion.

Photographer: **Kharen Hill**

The Air Plaza's *Flight Dream* became a night dream as the sun set each evening.

Photographer:
Rick Marotz

"I came to this world's fair because of the theme. I love transportation. I'm a jet pilot. My whole life, I've been fascinated with commercial forms of movement."
John Travolta, *Actor*, Los Angeles, California.

Photographer:
Peter Timmermans

"We're all volunteers from the Museum of Flight. I started as a mechanic for Canadian Airways, that was before CPA. I'm actually Canada's first licensed helicopter engineer. In those days you became part of the machine."
Art Limmert, Surrey, B.C.

Photographer:
Jürgen Vogt

133

● *Bottom Left*
_____

The Air Plaza featured *Flight Path*, a series of aircraft culminating in the nose of a Boeing 747 Jumbo Jet that soared 36 feet into the skies.

Photographer:
Stephe Tate

● *Bottom Right*
_____

Lifelike statues were strategically placed about the Air Plaza, lending a sense of human involvement to the flight celebration.

Photographer:
Peter Timmermans

CHILD'S PLAY AREA

● *Centre*

"This is great. My kids think this is the best part of Expo next to eating. They could stay here for all of our three days. Now there's an idea…"
Margaret Esson, Charlottetown, Prince Edward Island.

Photographer:
Thomas Bruckbauer

● *Top*

Photographer:
Gunter Marx

● *Bottom Left*

Photographer:
Rick Marotz

● *Bottom Right*

Photographer:
Perry Zavitz

ROYAL BANK / EXPO 86
WORLD FESTIVAL

● *Top*

"I decided not to touch the vehicles because I thought, if we started playing with it or sitting on the bikes, it would be using it as a toy almost. I wanted to use the energy, the sense of solitude that there is in it. For me, when *Highway 86* is empty, it has an incredible power."

Jean-Pierre Perrault, *Artistic Director— Highway 86 Dance Event,* Quebec City, Quebec.

Photographer:
Rick Marotz

● *Bottom*

In Celebration Of Whales featured not only the Vancouver Bach Choir under the direction of Bruce Pullen, but also seasoned performers Hyak, Bjossa and Finna of the Vancouver Aquarium.

Photographer:
Larry Goldstein

● *Facing Page*

Galantries, a very rare world premiere performed by Britain's renowned Royal Ballet.

Photographer:
Joseph Lederer

● *Top Left*

"How does a man dressed as a cart-horse build a windmill? He doesn't. He sings a song about it and, at the end of that song, there is a windmill half built by a stage crew. You have the mask of language, the visual mask on your face, the mask of music, the mask of the set. If you stay with the mask of metaphor, then the play can be."
Barry Rutter, *Actor-National Theatre of Great Britian*, London, England.
Photographer:
Glen Erikson

● *Bottom Left*

George Orwell's *Animal Farm* (National Theatre of Great Britain).
Photographer:
Glen Erikson

● *Bottom*

"When you realize what it takes to get a company like the Kirov here to perform, you know why they haven't come in 20-odd years. But when they dance, it's all worthwhile."
Ann Farris Darling, *Artistic Director—World Festival.*
Photographer:
Joseph Lederer

"The World Festival involvement has really been the crown of our whole presence at Expo. "From a personal standpoint, well, I've never really become involved in anything so deeply or enjoyed anything so much." **Dave Pollock,** *Vice President in charge of Expo—Royal Bank of Canada,* Vancouver, B.C.

The Dance Of The Benediction as performed by the Royal Thai Ballet July 22, Thailand National Day. Peaceful sentiments portrayed in dance epitomized the Thai presence at Expo.

Photographer:
Perry Zavitz

World-renowned Placido Domingo, featured in 'Antologia de la Zarzuela', an Iberian spectacular featuring a wide range of popular zarzuelas—partly spoken, partly sung melodies.

Photographer:
Joseph Lederer

The Beijing People's Art Theatre brought its acclaimed production of *Teahouse* to the World Festival. Three pivotal periods in modern Chinese history illustrated by the events in a teahouse, the play by Lao She took Expo audiences by storm.

Photographer:
Joseph Lederer

"The Ballet Gala features Canada's top three ballet companies with three premieres. And that's exciting.

"One premiere is an ambitious project, but to have three totally different ballets seen for the first time on the same night is quite an undertaking."
Valerie Wilder,
Artistic Director—

A rare glimpse of Royal Winnipeg Ballet members backstage during the world premiere of choreographer Brian MacDonald's *Steps*, part of the Ballet Gala.

Photographer:

An even rarer glimpse of an evening's shoes for Royal Winnipeg Ballet Prima Ballerina Evelyn Hart.

Photographer:
David Cooper

● *Facing Page*

The *Legong Keraton*, performed exclusively by adolescent girls, is the story of Good and Evil based on the epic Hindu poem—Ramayana. It represented Indonesia in the World Festival.

Photographer:
Gunter Marx

● *Following Pages*

"More than 850 costumes, 300 pairs of shoes, 150 wigs—11 containers that have everything inside. La Scala has truly moved to Vancouver!"
Sergio Escobar,
Assistant to the General Administrator—La Scala, Milan, Italy.

Photographer:
David Cooper

●

"Transferring La Scala here—the people and materials in such an amount—represents in itself the epitome of the Expo 86 theme.

"Its connection to Expo is that art is the most natural, the most enjoyable, the most instinctive form of human communication. "La Scala brought to us, in Vancouver, operatic art at its peak, at its most spectacular."
Piero B. Francese,
Deputy Commissioner General—Italy Pavilion.

● *Top*

Urban Sax from France brought a unique blend of ensemble music and performance art to the shores of False Creek July 7.

Photographer:
Gunter Marx

● *Bottom*

"The costumes don't really have any major significance. The music and the costumes go together and whatever the audience thinks...is what they mean. It's very personal."
Gilbert Artman,
Artistic Director—Urban Sax, France

Photographer:
Derik Murray

GREEN ZONE

MARINE PLAZA

● *Top Left*

"I was driving down Pacific Boulevard near the site and saw this elegant-looking crane and thought if we tied a couple of them together we could build a tall ship. Once we had the idea then Neale-Staniszkis Architects turned it into the *Dream Ship*, the focus of the Marine Plaza."
Bob McIlhargey, *Designer*, Vancouver B.C.

Photographer:
Jürgen Vogt

● *Bottom Left*

A replica of a tugboat bridge, replete with dials, switches and knobs for young hands to operate sat at one entrance to the Marine Plaza.

Photographer:
Edward M. Gifford

● *Top*

Photographer:
Peter Timmermans

● *Bottom*

"This is my favourite place on site. You'll never see so many boats from around the world again."
Bill Gordon, Seattle, Washington.

Photographer:
Peter Timmermans

● *Top*

Built for the movie, the HMS *Bounty* quickly became the star of the International Harbour during her stay.

Photographer:
Doane Gregory

● *Bottom Left*

"We found that running the *Bounty* was a lot like what they have here at Expo. It's a team, they have a voyage, and we have a voyage, except theirs is longer."
Colin Kesteven, HMS *Bounty*.

Photographer:
Barry Brooks

● *Bottom Right*

The stern of the mighty *Bounty* served as a reminder of the days of old when ships were more intricately decorated.

Photographer:
Gunter Marx

The *Golden Hinde*, a replica of Sir Francis Drake's 1579 warship, recalled a time when ships traversed the globe in search of new lands.

Photographer:
Ric Kokotovich

Master of the *Golden Hinde*, Dennis Ord.

Photographer:
Peter Timmermans

"I learned to sail with her, I was a landscape gardener before. I wanted to do something different."
Douglas Grossart,
Bosun—Golden Hinde.

Photographer:
Peter Timmermans

during the Exposition, an Indonesian Phinisi and a traditional York Boat.

Photographer:
Brent Daniels

Century as part of the Bugis people's ancestry.

Photographer:
Darryl Snaychuk

cracked over the hull rather than a bottle of champagne.

Photographer:
Jürgen Vogt

of every size and shape plied the waters of the Marine Plaza lagoon.

Photographer:
Gunter Marx

● *Top*

A hearty welcome could always be expected at the Alberta Pavilion. On May 19, Alberta Day, the welcome included a traditional chuckwagon breakfast.

Photographer:
Lloyd Sutton

● *Bottom*

The familiar white hats of the Calgary Stampede Show Band on Alberta Day.

Photographer:
Lloyd Sutton

● *Facing Page*

"Some days you just have to get out there and laugh. Last month we were climbing, we got to the top of the tower 10 stories above Expo...about a thousand people watching us. We're on a wooden climbing wall. Down below there are little model boats going by on a pond and at the same time a US spy plane was flying about 300 feet above us!" **Butch Greer**, *Lead Climber—Alberta Pavilion*, Calgary, Alberta.

Photographer:
Greg Athans

● *Top*

Helge Ingstad, famed ethnologist, visited the Great Norwegian Explorers exhibit. Ingstad was responsible for discovering the site of the first European settlement in North America—Vinland—which is a thousand years old this year.

Photographer:
Jürgen Vogt

● *Centre*

Known as great explorers of the sea since earliest days, the Norwegians showed their explorations below the seas for oil as well.

Photographer:
Brian Stablyk

● *Bottom*

Norway Day, May 29, was made all the more festive by the presence of Crown Prince Harald and Crown Princess Sonja at ceremonies celebrating the day and opening the Edvard Munch Exhibit at Vancouver Art Gallery.

Photographer:
Jürgen Vogt

● *Top Left*

Hungary Day, June 2, brought performances by the Kala Majka Folk Music Band

Photographer:
Kharen Hill

● *Top Right*

Belgium took the transportation theme to heart by displaying their famed cartoon character Tintin—the first man on the moon.

Photographer:
Darryl Snaychuk

● *Bottom Left*

Capping a sunny Barbados Day the Plaza of Nations erupted into a festival of colour and celebrations.

Photographer:
Kharen Hill

● *Bottom Right*

Costa Rica greeted Expo tourists with a giant postcard on their pavilion and a warm smile on their faces.

Photographer:
Doane Gregory.

●

"We've been going to Barbados for years now...every Christmas. I hate to admit it, I've learned more about the country at Expo than I have going there. Guess the sun kind of distracts you!"
Thelma Moberley,
Toronto, Ontario.

QUEBEC/
UNITED NATIONS

A far cry from the hustle and bustle of midday, the nighttime serenity of the Green Zone was a pleasure not to be missed.

Photographer:
Peter Timmermans

"I worked at Expo 67 as a student and had a great time. The people of Quebec are terrific and I really like their pavilion, and its theme—Quebec in motion, Quebec in contact."
Jeff Dryer, Calgary, Alberta.

Photographer:
Jürgen Vogt

● *Top*

"Each and every one of us has not only the responsibility and the obligation but also the right to let our voices be heard on behalf of those who are voiceless and to be heard in support of the causes that make a difference in how the human species conducts itself."
Harry Belafonte,
Singer,
New York, New York—Recording a message for peace at UN Pavilion.

Photographer:
Perry Zavitz

● *Centre*

Participants from pavilions recorded "Peace on Earth," an anthem written by Bruce Stacey.

Photographer:
Hans Sipma

● *Bottom*

"The painting symbolizes the way in which the United Nations serves in bringing the nations of the world together to foster greater human understanding and cooperation. The mural's title is *A World United*."
Paul Ygartua, *Mural Artist,* Vancouver, B.C.

Photographer:
Jürgen Vogt

PRINCE EDWARD ISLAND/ NOVA SCOTIA

● *Top*

Thanks to Canada's largest map, guests of the PEI Pavilion got a complete view of the island province.

Photographer:
Peter Timmermans

● *Centre Left*

Prince Edward Island— home of Canada's best- loved character, Anne Of Green Gables.

Photographer:
Larry Goldstein

● *Bottom Left*

"Cape Breton is absolutely beautiful, it's very, very beautiful. It's very special, especially to the people who were born there. Seems to draw you back. Once you leave, you don't stay away very long."
Rita MacNeil, *Singer,* Cape Breton, Nova Scotia.

Photographer:
Gunter Marx

● *Right*

Voices raised in songs from the mines, Nova Scotia's renowned Men of the Deeps celebrated 20 years as North America's only chorus of coal miners in 1986.

Photographer:
Gunter Marx

● *Top*

"This is a very special year for Air Canada. It's our fiftieth anniversary and the airplane that made history for us is inside our pavilion—the Lockheed 10A. That was the very first aircraft that Air Canada owned. It flew fifty years ago today, as a matter of fact—September 1— from Vancouver to Seattle."
Paul LeBlanc,
Host—Air Canada Pavilion,
Vancouver, B.C.

Photographer:
Kharen Hill

● *Bottom*

"Being in the photography industry I really enjoyed the audio-visual displays in the pavilions. I've learned a lot."
Patrick Morrow, *Grand Slam Mountaineer,*
Kimberley, B.C.

Photographer:
Kharen Hill

High above the Green
Zone, the Air Canada
Gondola provided a
matchless view.

Photographer:
Derik Murray

The first powered
aircraft in the British
Empire, *The Silver Dart*,
hung above the crowds
waiting to enter the Air
Canada Pavilion.

Photographer:
Albert Chin

● *Top*

"The big beauty of Expo for me is the people-watching and all the various foods. I tried to nibble at all the counters…"
Barry Rutter, London, England.

Photographer:
Jürgen Vogt

● *Bottom Left*

Authentic ethnic entertainment wasn't confined to just stages and theatres at Expo.

Photographer:
Stephe Tate

● *Bottom Right*

It was hard to say *auf wiedersehen* to the traditional Bavarian Garden.

Photographer:
Peter Timmermans

Fanfare for France
National Day much as
it was performed for
Napoleon in the early
19th Century.

Photographer:
Rick Marotz

Metro's Louvre Station.

Photographer:
Albert Normandin

The France Pavilion was a brightly coloured and very interactive display of technology.

Photographer:
Anna Beaudry

On France National Day, held July 7 (Bastille Day), a replica of the 200-year-old Montgolfier brothers hot air balloon flew above the Expo site.

Photographer:
Jürgen Vogt

Operated by the Société Nationale des Chemins de Fers—French National Railways, the TGV is the ultimate in rail transport.

Photographer:
Albert Normandin

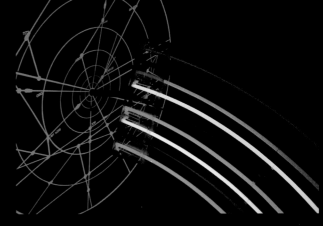

● *Top Left*

Bringing together 12 member states, the European Economic Community Pavilion rounded out the European presence.

Photographer:
Larry Goldstein

● *Bottom Left*

"I think EXPO 86 was a very bold idea, very boldly carried out and I believe it exceeded all expectations."
Margaret Thatcher, *Prime Minister—Great Britain,* London, England.

Photographer:
Peter Timmermans

● *Bottom*

"You know, it doesn't matter how long you've been away...You'll always miss living there."
Audrey Torrance, Windsor, Ontario.

Photographer:
Patrick Morrow

The *Optica* observation aircraft impressed guests with its unusual design. It boasts 270 degree visibility and runs at one-quarter the cost of a comparable single-turbine helicopter.

Photographer:
Peter Timmermans

A bit of the spirit of the British Isles could be found in every glass tapped in the Captain George Vancouver Pub in the British Pavilion.

Photographer:
Brian Stablyk

A stunning array of Jaguars, Lotuses, Rolls Royces and other well-known British contributions to automotive transport.

Photographer:
Michael Morissette

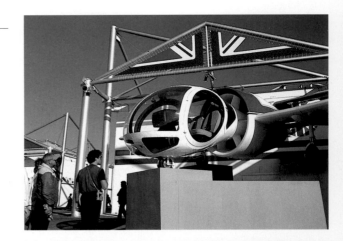

FEDERAL REPUBLIC OF GERMANY

● *Top*

The Duo bus, prominent in the German Pavilion, has the capability of running on diesel or electricity thanks to a pair of engines.

Photographer:
Vlado Matisic

● *Bottom Left*

A tradition in Germany enjoyed by young and old, Henry the Organ Grinder welcomed people to the German Pavilion at Expo.

Photographer:
Rick Marotz

● *Bottom Right*

Several examples of Germany's famed Mercedes Benz autos were on display, including the classic 1927 600 Model K open tourer.

Photographer:
Stuart N. Dee

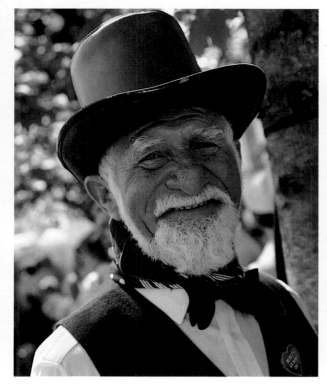

● *Top*

Women of the Royal
H███ Kong Police
Department performed
the traditional Ribbon
Dance on Hong Kong
Day, July 18.

Photographer:
Jürgen Vogt

● *Bottom*

The Hong Kong
Pavilion, on closer
examination, was
covered in bamboo
scaffolding. Live
workers joined the
statues throughout
Expo, altering the
design.

Photographer:
Ric Kokotovich

● *Top*

Women of the Royal
H███ Kong Police
Department performed
the traditional Ribbon
Dance on Hong Kong
Day, July 18.

Photographer:
Jürgen Vogt

● *Bottom*

The Hong Kong
Pavilion, on closer
examination, was
covered in bamboo
scaffolding. Live
workers joined the
statues throughout
Expo, altering the
design.

Photographer:
Ric Kokotovich

● *Top*

"I can do 40 of these caricatures in an hour. Yes, they call me the fastest draw in the East."
Bill Yim, *cartoonist,* Hong Kong.

Photographer:
Stuart N. Dee

● *Bottom*

Students from St. Catherine's School for Girls drew postcards for visitors on Hong Kong Day, all part of the pavilion theme—"Hong Kong In Touch With The World."

Photographer:
Jürgen Vogt

ROUNDHOUSE

● *Facing Page*

Built to last—rebuilt to stay, the Roundhouse was Vancouver's first industrial building and home to an eclectic collection of transportation inventions during Expo.

Photographer:
William P. McElligott

● *Top*

Standing stately in the Roundhouse courtyard was Locomotive #374, which delivered the first transcontinental passengers to Vancouver in 1887.

Photographer:
Perry Zavitz

● *Centre*

A 26-foot-high locomotive driving wheel stood inside the old diesel shop.

Photographer:
Stuart N. Dee

● *Bottom*

Performers from Czechoslovakia's Art Centrum circled the Roundhouse on aerial tracks, demonstrating the eccentric human-powered vehicles on display.

Photographer:
Doane Gregory

Employed by Imperial Oil 30 years ago and now retired, Al Sholund and wife Nellie helped guests find names on Heritage Bricks in the Roundhouse Courtyard.

Photographer:
Jürgen Vogt

As animated as the crazy inventions, the performers from Art Centrum were constantly in motion.

Photographer:
Doane Gregory

The largest collection of holograms ever assembled amazed visitors to *The Spectral Image,* thanks to Canadian artist Michael Snow.

Photographer:
Michel Pilon

● *Top Left*

Warmth and goodwill were always in evidence as Italy welcomed the world to its pavilion.

Photographer:
Doane Gregory

● *Top Right*

Naturally, the famed Ferrari—symbol of Italian excellence in design—was featured at the Italy Pavilion.

Photographer:
Jürgen Vogt

● *Centre Left*

A world leader in superior automotive technology, Italy showed the promise of the future as well as the legacy of the past.

● *Bottom Left*

July 28 was Spain National Day at EXPO 86.

Photographer:
Gunter Marx

● *Bottom Right*

Spain, the host of the 1992 Universal Exposition at Seville.

Photographer:
Edward M. Gifford

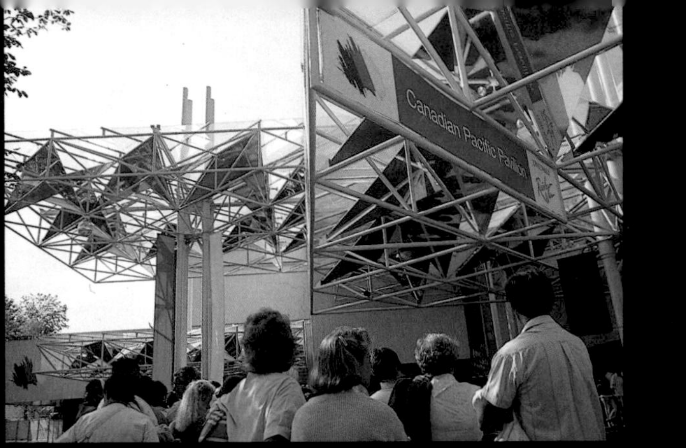
Canadian Pacific Pavilion

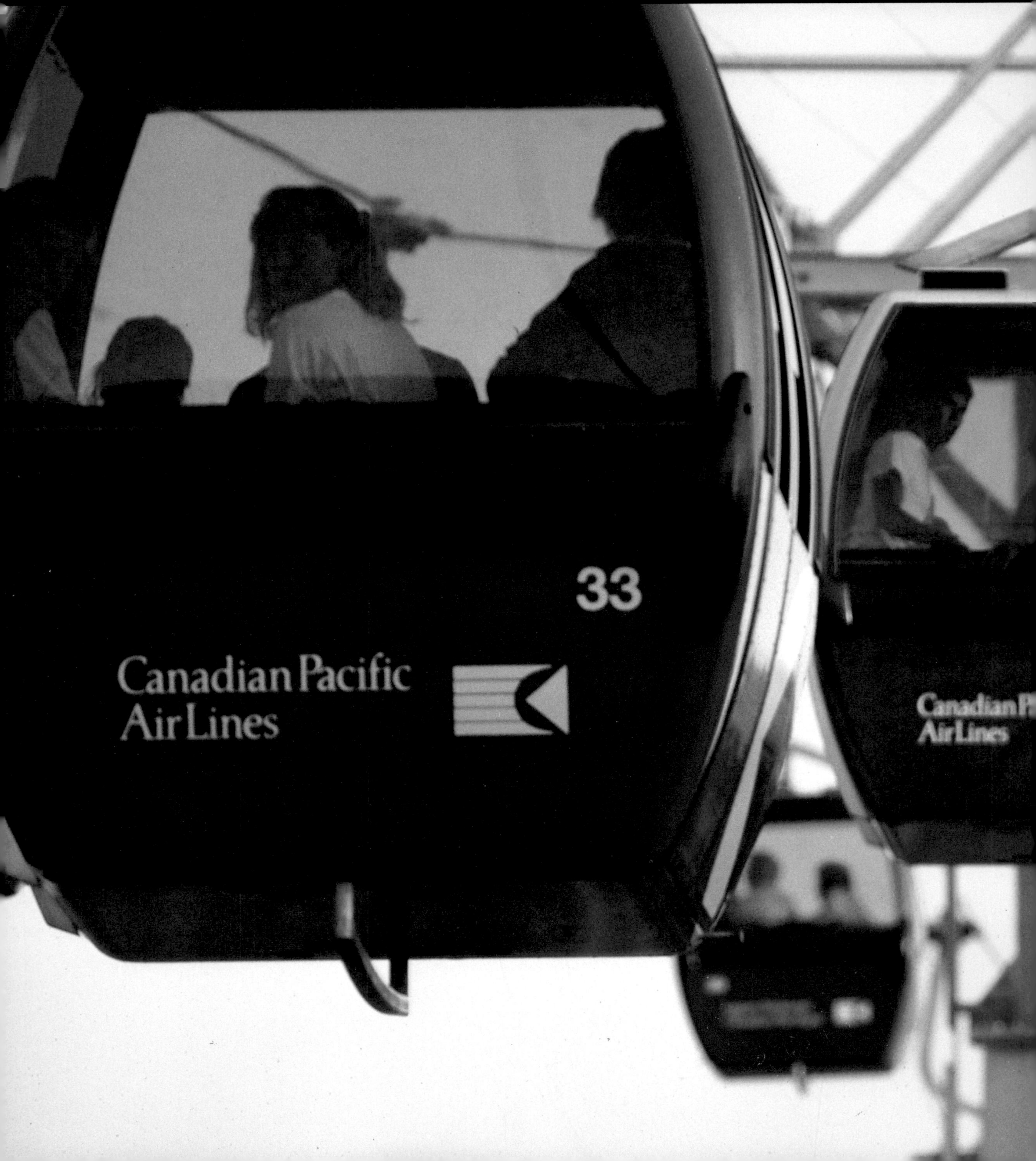
33
Canadian Pacific
Air Lines

The Canadian Pacific Pavilion served as a stage for three presentations. Most popular amongst them was the Academy Award-nominated *Rainbow War*.

Photographer:
Norm Stelfox

The 67-gondola Canadian Pacific Skyride carried the colours of one of the official airlines of EXPO 86.

Photographer:
Rick Marotz

"By choosing to present *Rainbow War*, Canadian Pacific are sort of offering an olive branch. They're saying, 'Look, we know how to get around now, we know how to transport each other. If we're all going to survive and prosper together we'd better figure out how to get along with each other.'"
Bob Rogers,
Producer—Rainbow War,
Los Angeles, California.

● *Bottom*

The Vancouver International Puppetfest brought artists together in a spirit of celebration throughout the site.

Photographer:
Kharen Hill

● *Top Right*

Everyone got a healthy dose of the magic elixir of youth on International Children's Day, June 1.

Photographer:
Gunter Marx

● *Bottom Right*

Beaux Gestes '86 turned the walkways and theatres of Expo into a moving feast of mime, clown and movement theatre from all over the globe.

Photographer:
Kharen Hill

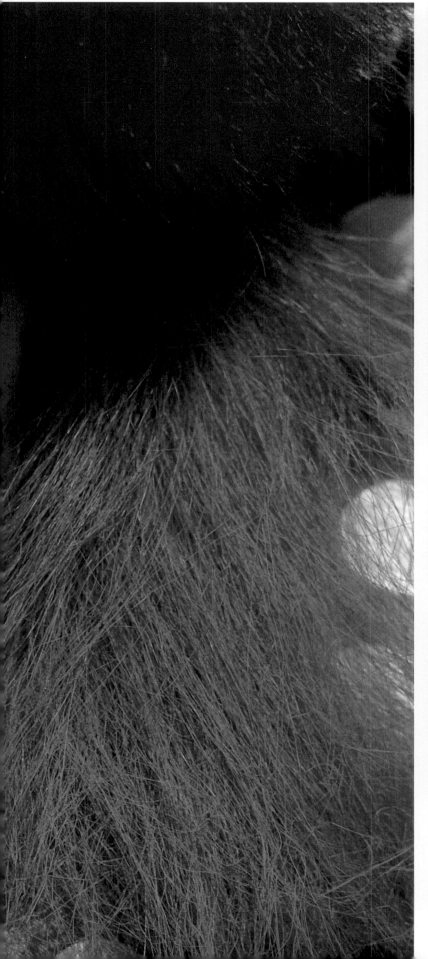

● *Top*

Fourteen thousand
performances were given
on the streets and
walkways throughout
Expo—performances
such as those by Jean
Filion and Soizick
Hébèrt of Quebec's
Les Voilà.

Photographer:
Brian Stablyk

● *Bottom*

Garbo's Garbage
Pavilion was a surprise
to all. You never knew
where he was going to
turn up or what he
might do to amuse and
delight.

Photographer:
Jürgen Vogt

● *Facing Page*

"I'm the smallest
pavilion here. See,
I've got a passport
stamp and everything!"
Fred Garbo, *Street
Performer,* Norway,
Maine.

Photographer:
Peter Timmermans

On-Site
Entertainment

GARBOS'
GARBAGE
PAVILION

● *Facing Page*

Michel Jodoin, founder of Espace Michel Jodoin from Quebec.

Photographer:
Kharen Hill

● *Top Left*

"They were great. You can't tell them from the real staff. Well, maybe that's not quite true..."
Rick Turner, Seattle, Washington.
Line-up Maintenance Crew from BC and Alberta.

Photographer:
Norm Stelfox

● *Centre Left*

Vancouver's Special Delivery Dance Music Theatre.

Photographer:
Gunter Marx

● *Centre Right*

Mark Wenzel of San Diego, California.

Photographer:
Jane Weitzel

● *Bottom Left*

Smart Star, one of the five Promenauts at the Canada Pavilion brought the charm of street theatre to the high tech theme of EXPO 86.

Photographer:
Albert Normandin

● *Bottom Right*

Gerard Devine, 'Red the Juggler,' from Vancouver.

Photographer:
Albert Normandin

● *Top*

"We're having a ball here. It's our day!"
Gloria McPhadden,
Regina, Saskatchewan.

Photographer:
Jürgen Vogt

● *Centre*

Nancy Garland,
Dragon Sherman and
Karen Weseloh from
San Diego.

Photographer:
Anna Beaudry

● *Bottom Left*

Obvious enjoyment in
the Yellow Zone.

Photographer:
Lloyd Sutton

● *Bottom Right*

Something for everyone.

Photographer:
Kharen Hill

Large murals, depicting the transportation and communications theme of Expo, decorated the walkways.
"Reach out and touch some nuns..."
David Grierson,
Vancouver, B.C.

Photographer:
Peter Timmermans

David Chantler of Alberta's Trickster Theatre Company.

Photographer:
Peter Timmermans

Boy Scouts of America, prepared for a day of adventure.

Photographer:
Janis Kraulis

Sharing the soundtrack for a day at Expo.

Photographer:
Peter Timmermans

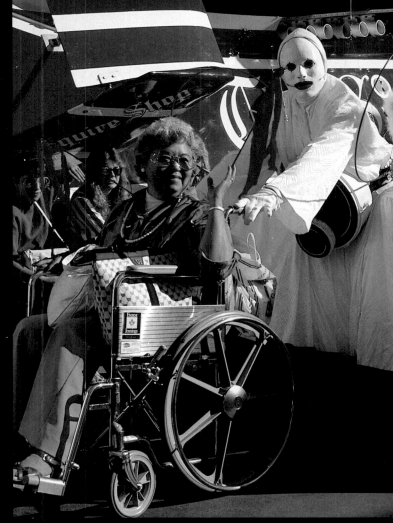

●

"If you haven't got a sense of humour on this site you wouldn't survive. There're so many people, so many different kinds of people, so many things that happen."
Bill Neill,
Director—Service Operations, EXPO 86, Vancouver, B.C.

YELLOW ZONE

KODAK PACIFIC
BOWL

● *Top*

"I think people forget sometimes that the actual performance of the Musical Ride is only a part of what we do. Each one of our performances is only 25 minutes and a few odd seconds long but we're down here for four hours. That's four hours in which we have a chance to interact with people that are coming through and asking questions.

"Being on the Musical Ride is a little bit like having 30 brothers and 2 sisters."

Vern Baugh, *Officer in Charge—1986* RCMP *Musical Ride,* Edmonton, Alberta.

Photographer:
Jürgen Vogt

● *Bottom*

The Kodak Pacific Bowl, a 5,000-seat outdoor grandstand and arena, was host to hundreds of performances, ceremonies and displays.

Photographer:
Edward M. Gifford

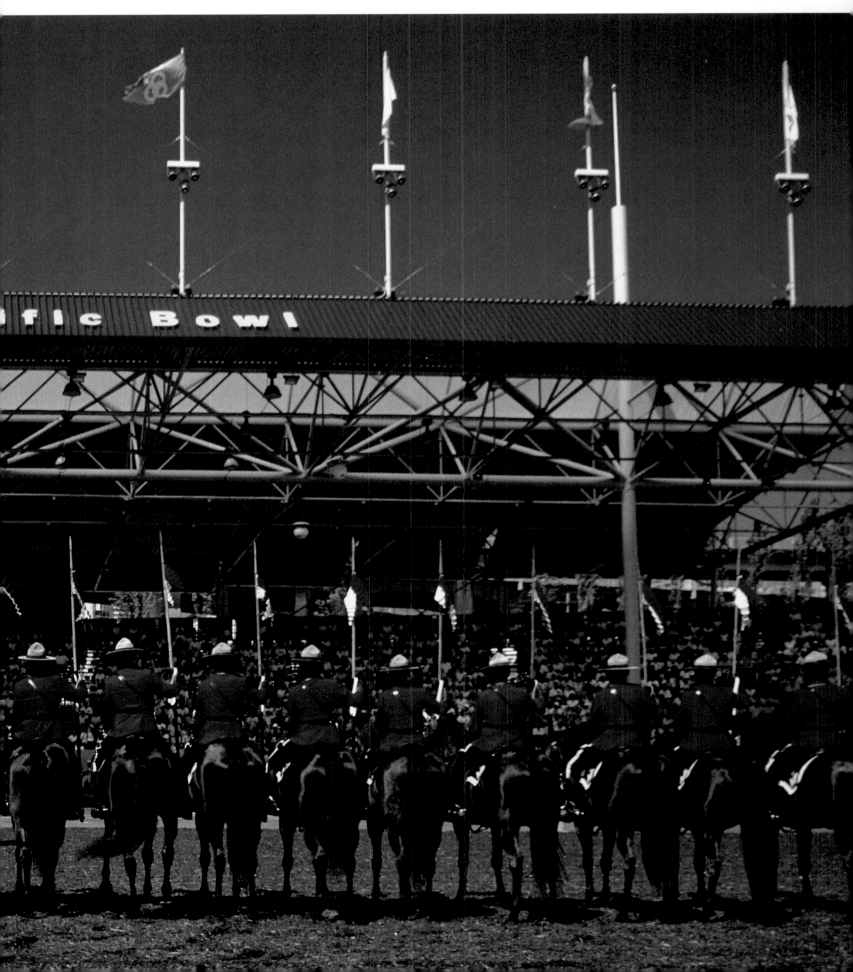

● *Top*

"We saw the policemen on the horses. They were big and they were going to hit each other. But they didn't."
Peter Hrynkow, *age 3*, Vancouver, B.C.

Photographer:
Edward M. Gifford

● *Bottom Left*

Formed 110 years ago to break the monotony of the cold northern winters, the RCMP Concert Band's numerous Expo appearances brightened the hot summer days.

Photographer:
Gunter Marx

● *Bottom Right*

The Musical Ride took up residence at EXPO 86 for the duration of the exposition, the longest they've stayed anywhere outside Ottawa.

Photographer:
Rick Marotz

● *Facing Page*

The thrill and spectacle of the RCMP Musical Ride was enough to make anyone aspire to a career in red serge.

Photographer:
Jürgen Vogt

Top

Started by the British Army in the 16th Century as a way of bringing villagers back into the safety of the fort at night, the Sunset Ceremony or Beating of Retreat signalled an end to Britain Day at Expo.

Photographer:
Jürgen Vogt

Centre

"Those guys really whiz around in there. You'd think they'd just spin out the top, but they don't!"
Mark Smigelski,
Lethbridge, Alberta.

Photographer:
Jürgen Vogt

Bottom Left

From the People's Republic of China, the Kaifeng Motorcycle Team defied death with every performance at Kodak Pacific Bowl.

Photographer:
Jürgen Vogt

Bottom Right

Canada Day, July 1, the Kodak Pacific Bowl was the focal point for celebrations. The RCMP Musical Ride, the Nylons, The Snowbirds, wheelchair athlete Rick Hansen via satellite and thousands of guests wished Canada a happy 119th birthday.

Photographer:
Jane Weitzel

The skirl of the pipes and the tossing of the caber were just part of the Scottish Festival at Kodak Pacific Bowl in July.

Photographer:
Lloyd Sutton

The human chess game of Marostica came to Expo from Italy, bringing costumes, banners, and performers. They recruited an additional 150 extras from the local Italian community.

Photographer:
Derik Murray

Marostica's chess board was as neatly ordered as their performance schedule at home in Italy: every second Friday, Saturday and Sunday during September of only even years.

Photographer:
Rick Marotz

"I always thought chess was slow and a little boring, but this changes things entirely."
Geoff Massey,
Houston, Texas.

Photographer:
Derik Murray

● *Top*

"I think that Telecom made me feel very proud to be a Canadian. They portrayed Canada very well."
Jill Edgar,
Vancouver, B.C.

Photographer:
Hans Sipma

● *Bottom*

Telecom Canada highlighted the many technological aspects of the communications consortium. They capped it off with a friendly smile at every turn.

Photographer:
Hans Sipma

MALAYSIA/
COTE D'IVOIRE/
CUBA/
KOREA

● *Top Left*

Malaysia gave the visitor a truly personal sense of its country and people through an audio-visual display, exhibits and congenial staff.

Photographer:
John Kenny

● *Top Right*

Nayanka Bell, a national treasure, accompanied by her group of dancers, entertained for Côte D'Ivoire Day July 15.

Photographer:
Jürgen Vogt

● *Bottom Left*

Expo guests snapped up the hand-rolled Cuban cigars. "Many people take this for granted, but it's a very fine thing ..passed from one generation to another." **Isabel Bejarano,** *Cigar Roller—Cuba Pavilion,* Havana, Cuba.

Photographer:
John Kenny

● *Bottom Right*

Dressed in their national colours for Korea Day, spectators watched a performance of Samul Nori.

Photographer:
Jürgen Vogt

● *Top*

The Great Hall of
Ramses II. Treasures
from 3,000 years ago
were displayed for Expo
guests and explained by
helpful guides.

Photographer:
Edward M. Gifford

● *Facing Page*

"In the doing of
buildings there are
different responsibilities.
For example, at the
level of Ramses what we
were dealing with was
the art of man; a bit of
history; magnificent
sculptures that went
back several thousand
years.
"Putting that in an
appropriate setting is
the name of the game.
It was almost pure
theatre."
Allan Waisman,
*Architect—Waisman
Dewar Grout Carter,*
Vancouver, B.C.

Photographer:
Lloyd Sutton

● *Bottom Left*

"We shouldn't forget
that the pyramids and
many of the major
temples we still have in
Egypt today were over a
thousand years old at
the time when Ramses
was a young boy. He
was a tourist visiting
the pyramids."
Mark Simpkins,
Egyptologist, Salt Lake
City, Utah.

Photographer:
Albert Normandin

● *Bottom Right*

Powerful and quite
prolific, Ramses' family
were often captured in
ornate likenesses.

Photographer:
Albert Normandin

● *Top*

The space shuttle—the crowning achievement of the US manned space program—was the highlight of the film presentation in the US Pavilion. The impressive display captured the imagination of Expo visitors.

Photographer:
Brian Stablyk

● *Bottom Left*

A skywalk simulated changes in environment as guests entered the US Pavilion. Once inside, the wonders of space were close at hand.

Photographer:
Rick Marotz

● *Bottom Right*

The potential for future innovation in space was evident in the display of Space Station technology.

Photographer:
Rick Marotz

● *Top*

"Yes, it's the fourth of July and yes, I'm an American and yes, I'm away from home and I miss it. But it's still the Fourth of July!"
Chris Manson, San Diego, California.

Photographer:
Jürgen Vogt

● *Centre*

Massive vessels docked in the harbour and a great contingent of sailors on shore meant an Independance Day with considerable significance.

Photographer:
Jürgen Vogt

● *Top*

"I have to admit, after a day of walking, this pavilion is really a treat. You let them do the walking for you with this people mover thing."
Marjorie Kupton, Ottawa, Ontario.

Photographer:
Jürgen Vogt

● *Bottom*

Balletacoma, one of Washington State's entertainment highlights at Expo.

Photographer:
Jürgen Vogt

●

"The Second Century, the Century of Promise" was the theme of the Washington State Pavilion at Expo. A strong kinship is felt between this state and B.C. as they adjoin the international border and share many cultural and trade links.

With a fanfare from a band and dignitaries present, Oregon State celebrated its day, May 24.

Photographer:
Michael Morissette

A cascading waterfall, a 21st Century representation of a covered wagon, and exhibits of the life and commerce of Oregon made theirs a pavilion of constant change and delight.

Photographer:
Stuart N. Dee

Logging, one of Oregon's prime industries, brought an entertaining focus to Oregon Day.

Photographer:
Michael Morissette

● Top

Featured most prominently in the California Pavilion was the 10,000-pound Apollo XIV capsule— *Kitty Hawk.* "We are creating the future." **George Deukmejian,** *Governor, State of California,* Sacramento, California.

Photographer: **Stuart N. Dee**

● Bottom Left

The California Pavilion was an active one with lots to do—including playing with these plasma globes which appeared to have lightning trapped inside.

Photographer: **Lloyd Sutton**

● Bottom Right

The famed California tan shown to best advantage on California Day, August 6.

Photographer: **Jürgen Vogt**

Towering above the West Gate Plaza, *Rowingbridge* brought worlds together in a celebration of form and movement. Elements of a Japanese ceremonial gateway and the obvious boat imagery made it an ever-fascinating and ever-changing sculpture. "It's moving, on one hand, but stationary on the other. It would seem to me that it rows away, but it doesn't row through space at all. It's rowing through time."
Geoffrey Smedley, *Sculptor*, Gambier Island, B.C.

Photographer:
Stuart N. Dee

IBM EXPO INFO, state-of-the-art computer technology made accessible all over the site to guests. Millions of questions were posed daily, never without an answer in return.

Photographer:
Albert Chin

A huge steel bird, *Spirit Catcher* was created by Ontario sculptor Ron Baird.

Photographer:
Jürgen Vogt

The wedge shape of the General Motors Pavilion was unique at the Exposition. "We called the pavilion a 'motion wedge' and everyone's picked that up. It's just that simple. Instantly you know it's GM and it's got a tinge of motion."

Clive Grout, *Architect — Waisman Dewar Grout Carter.* Vancouver, B.C.

Photographer:
Peter Timmermans

The auto explored, at General Motors Pavilion.

Photographer:
Rick Marotz

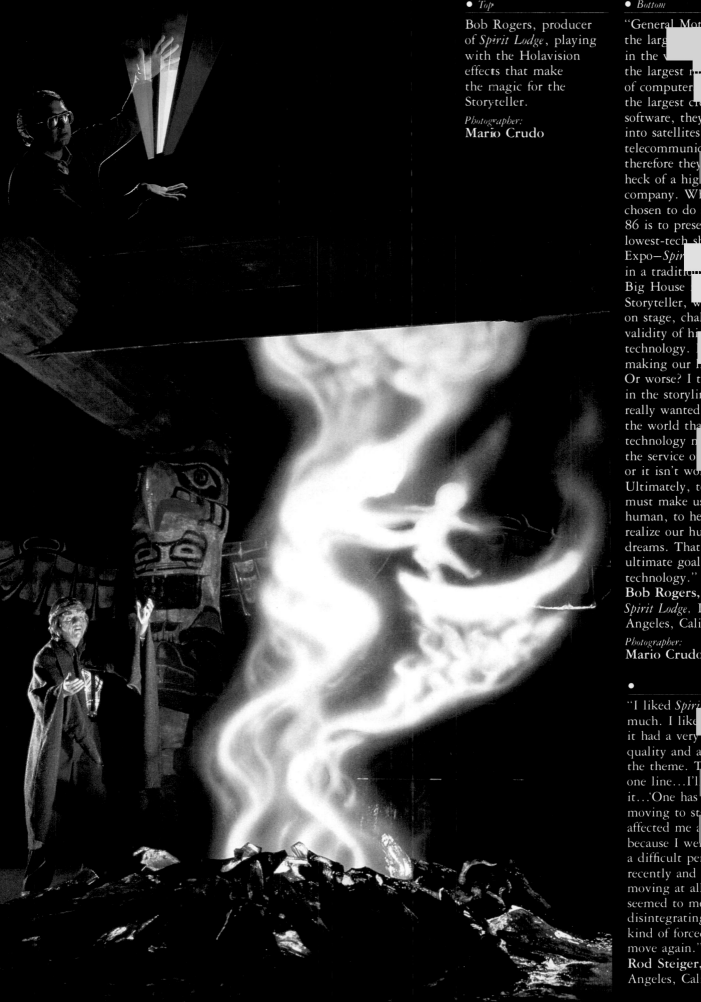

Bob Rogers, producer of *Spirit Lodge*, playing with the Holavision effects that make the magic for the Storyteller.

Photographer:
Mario Crudo

"General Motors is the largest corporation in the world. They are the largest manufacturer of computers, one of the largest creators of software, they are into satellites and telecommunication and therefore they are one heck of a high-tech company. What they've chosen to do at EXPO 86 is to present the lowest-tech show at Expo—*Spirit Lodge*—set in a traditional Indian Big House in which the Storyteller, who appears on stage, challenges the validity of high technology. Is it making our lives better? Or worse? I think that in the storyline GM really wanted to say to the world that technology must be in the service of humanity or it isn't worth it. Ultimately, technology must make us more human, to help us realize our human dreams. That is the ultimate goal of technology."
Bob Rogers, *Producer—Spirit Lodge.* Los Angeles, California.

Photographer:
Mario Crudo

●

"I liked *Spirit Lodge* very much. I liked it because it had a very real quality and also liked the theme. There was one line…I'll paraphrase it…'One has to keep moving to stay alive.' It affected me a great deal because I went through a difficult period recently and I wasn't moving at all. It seemed to me I was disintegrating and I kind of forced myself to move again."
Rod Steiger, *Actor.* Los Angeles, California.

XEROX
INTERNATIONAL
THEATRE

● *Top*

Six couples, five from Canada and one from the US, were married in traditional Japanese Shinto ceremonies at the Xerox International Theatre.

Photographer:
Lloyd Sutton

● *Bottom Left*

"I think what we were looking for was something away from the Canadian traditional ceremony—the standard walk up the aisle and first dance. I think we were looking for a different type of tradition. Something like this. We're never going to forget this."
Patrick Martin and Dorri Fahlen, *Bride and Groom,* Edmonton, Alberta

Photographer:
Joe Lederer

● *Facing Page*

Members of the Ikuta Shinto Shrine Performing Arts Group took part in the weddings at the Xerox International Theatre.

Photographer:
Gunter Marx

● *Bottom Right*

A folkloric ritual, the Shinto weddings only took half an hour to perform but hours of preparation. They involved about 50 priests, musicians, dancers and shrine maidens.

Photographer:
Gunter Marx

The Torres Strait Islanders Dance Group from Australia brought cheerful music to the sunny days at Expo.

Photographer:
Norm Stelfox

The hottest thing up and down the coast of West Africa, Youssou N'Dour electrified Xerox International Theatre audiences with their very special brand of Senegalese music.

Photographer:
Derik Murray

Korean heritage in dance, dialogue, gesture and song. The Pongsan Mask Dance Drama Troupe were one of the inaugural performance groups in the theatre.

Photographer:
Gunter Marx

● *Top*

Using indigenous instruments, the National Performing Arts Group of Pakistan play to audiences the world over.

Photographer:
Norm Stelfox

● *Bottom Left*

Backstage with a Canadian legend in country and rock and roll music. Ronnie Hawkins had the Xerox International Theatre "a 'rockin' with The Hawk!"

Photographer:
Darryl Snaychuk

● *Bottom Right*

On the cutting edge of contemporary dance, Ch Tanztheatre from Switzerland were truly remarkable.

Photographer:
Jürgen Vogt

"In the singing every word has a meaning. Dancing has a word and meaning. Not only just dancing, not only just singing for fun. It brings you a feeling of looking back into the past."
Wandjuk Kalkurru *(Aborigine Performer),* Arnemland, Northern Territory, Australia.

Photographer:
John Kalkurru (directed by Derik Murray)

New York's Murray Louis Dance Company performed at the Xerox International Theatre.

Photographer:
Stuart N. Dee

"Those Bloolips guys were just hilarious. Can you call them guys, dressed like that?"
Mark Dalton, Toronto, Ontario.

Photographer:
Peter Timmermans

BRITISH COLUMBIA TELEVISION

● *Top*

BCTV's News Hour boasts the largest English-speaking audience of any newscast in Canada.

Photographer:
Brian Stablyk

● *Bottom Left*

British Columbia Television, an affiliate of the CTV Network, moved their entire newsroom to Expo.

Photographer:
Peter Timmermans

● *Bottom Right*

"Communication...that's what we're all about and it's basically what the exposition's all about. I think most people come through here wondering why we're here. How we fit in to transportation and so on. But once they get in and they see all these displays it suddenly dawns on them 'Yeah,

that's what these guys do every day. Communicate.'
Tony Parsons, *Newscaster,* with **Pamela Martin,** *Newscaster—* BCTV *Pavilion,* Vancouver, B.C.

Photographer:
Larry Goldstein

DIVE TANK/
CARIBOU LOG
CHUTE/
MINOLTA SPACE
TOWER

● *Top*

The view from inside the Dive Tank in the Yellow Zone. Daily demonstrations in the Dive Tank included everything from underwater safety to sports to a wedding!

Photographer:
Mike Paris

● *Facing Page*

"You wouldn't get me in one of those capsule things. Those are for the kids. But the ride up in the observatory is wonderful, especially at night with the lights."
Hazel Matheson,
Seattle, Washington

Photographer:
Edward M. Gifford

● *Following Pages*

"Once in awhile you have to wait for a long time to get on the monorail. It's very popular, but you get such a great view of the pavilions and everything."
Terry Mattson,
Victoria, B.C.

Photographer:
Rick Marotz

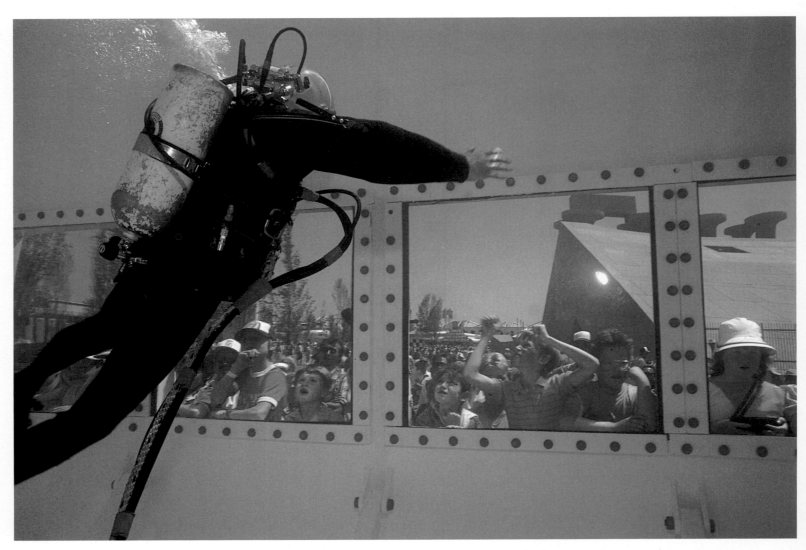

● *Bottom*

"It's wonderful! It's wild! It's wicked! It's whoopee! It's wet! So am I!"
Ambrose Fletcher,
age 13, Eugene, Oregon.

Photographer:
Norm Stelfox

"We made a mistake by only booking ourselves in for three days. We should have stayed the week. Bravo! Chapeau! It's a huge success!"
Michael York, *Actor,*
Paris, France.

Photographer:
Jürgen Vogt

"As one photographer on this project put it so well, Expo for him was a movie. Continually changing, no scene the same, constantly seen through the viewfinder of a camera. That creative perspective gave this book the magic we believe it to have. Our thanks to those whose photographs and stories appear on the following pages. You were all a distinct pleasure to work with."

The Expo
Celebration

THE PHOTOGRAPHERS

Greg Athans
A former world-class athlete as well as photographer, Athans is the holder of 4 world freestyle skiing titles and 15 national water-ski titles. He runs his own studio in downtown Vancouver, where he specializes in product photography for a variety of clients.

Anna Beaudry
Only 23 years of age and entirely self-taught, Beaudry captured the gold medal for promotional photography at the 1986 International Graphics Awards. She is a specialist in people and products, and has her own studio in Ottawa, Ontario, the nation's capital.

Roger Brooks
A civil engineer turned photographer four years ago, Brooks is uniquely qualified as one of Vancouver's top architectural photographers. He found the chance to work extensively in 35mm for this book a welcome relief from the rigidity of large format photography.

Albert Chin
For Chin, it was a choice between being an architect or a photographer. Obviously, the world behind the camera won. He pursued his studies at the University of British Columbia and today shoots primarily for stock, annual reports and audio-visual projects.

David Cooper
Cooper is recognized as one of the nation's leading dance and theatre photographers, working for the Stratford Festival and Shaw Festival, and the Royal Winnipeg Ballet, as well as many performing groups in his home town of Vancouver. He works out of his Yaletown studio.

Heather Dean
This native Vancouverite has specialized in aerial, location and people photography for the past six years. A self-taught artist, Dean's work has appeared in both local and national consumer magazines. The year 1986 has proven to be the most eventful yet in Dean's career.

Stuart N. Dee
Coming to Vancouver from the Philippines 14 years ago, Dee is a graduate in Fine Arts from the University of British Columbia. While he's an eight-year veteran of the commercial field, today he divides his time between his commercial work and fine art photography.

Nigel Dickson
Born in jolly England 37 years ago, Toronto's Dickson claims to have blue eyes, grey hair and "zero education." Among his other credits are numerous awards, portraits of Canada's last four prime ministers and being thrown out of more bars than he cares to remember.

Glen Erikson
Erikson has run his photography and graphic design studio in Vancouver for 12 years, working primarily in live arts, entertainment and public relations. His portfolio features work for the Arts Club Theatre, City Stage and the Vancouver Symphony Orchestra.

Edward M. Gifford
Gifford studied art and photography at the University of New Mexico, graduating in 1971. Since then he has worked as a freelance location photographer and educator. He's also the co-founder of Creo³, a non-profit art gallery and resource centre for photographers.

Larry Goldstein
Goldstein's work has appeared in several publications including *Western Living, Equity, Your Money, Dial* and *Vancouver Magazine*. Born in Montreal, he has been involved in photography for the past 10 years and enjoys advertising work as well as editorial photography.

David Gray
Originally of Winston-Salem, North Carolina, Gray moved to Los Angeles in 1978 to study photography and film-making at Art Center College of Design. In 1982, he brought his many talents to Vancouver where he's earned an enviable reputation in the commercial field.

Doane Gregory
While he's based in Vancouver, Gregory's photographic art has been exhibited on both sides of the 49th Parallel and it resides in collections in seven countries. His editorial work can also be found with increasing regularity in a number of Canadian and American magazines.

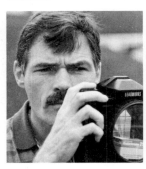

Al Harvey
Al Harvey is recognized for having one of the best appetites in Western Canada. This Vancouver native eats, drinks and sleeps audio-visual and corporate location photography. In addition, he maintains an extensive "Slide Farm where Kodachrome is always in season."

Tim Harvey
Winner of the 1986 Western Magazine Award for fashion editorial and numerous Graphex Awards over the years, Harvey has established himself as one of Canada's leading fashion and portrait photographers. His work is often seen in B.C. and national publications.

Kharen Hill
Hill is a New Zealander/Canadian who has photographed in Europe, Asia, India, North America and the Caribbean. She works largely in the audio-visual field though her work has appeared in many publications including *Architectural Digest* and *Art Post*.

Ron Holmes
Working as a photographer and audio-visual producer, Holmes has a strong personal interest in dance and "international cultural exchange in the Performing Arts." He is a graduate of the Media Resources Program at Capilano College, North Vancouver.

John Kenny
New York, Paris and now Vancouver, all have been home to fashion free-lancer John Kenny. A graduate of Art Center and former assistant to Steven Meisel and Irving Penn, he has garnered assignments for the likes of *W, M, The New York Times* and *American Vogue*.

Ric Kokotovich
Currently working in Calgary, Kokotovich first exhibited his art in New York City in 1982. He is known for choosing subjects of a different and amusing nature, as in his *Mardi Gras* series which features the notorious, New Orleans "Fat Tuesday" Parade.

Janis A. Kraulis
The photographer, writer and/or editor of a dozen picture books, Kraulis is best known for his wilderness and landscape work, though he has several areas of expertise. His most recent project, *The Rocky Mountains/Crest of a Continent*, will be published in Fall 1986.

Joseph Lederer
One of the city's top still photographers, "Foto-Jo" has worked on films such as *First Blood, Rocky IV, Star 80, Clan of the Cave Bear, The Boy Who Could Fly* and *The Stepfather*. He also operates a commercial studio for his corporate and advertising clients.

Dee Lippingwell
After 14 years of shooting rock stars, Lippingwell's work has appeared in publications virtually everywhere in the world and she herself has appeared in the *Canadian Who's Who of Women*. She has two goals in life: to keep her sense of humour and find parking at Expo.

Rick Marotz
A veteran of over 30 years in the art of creative photography, Marotz says "the biggest asset for a photographer is patience." His award-winning photos appear in magazines such as *Beautiful B.C., Maclean's* and *Time*. Some of his works are in the National Film Board Still Library.

Gunter Marx
While a Vancouver resident since 1965, Marx has exhibited his work throughout Canada, the U.S.A., Mexico and Europe, winning several awards in the process. His main interest in photography lies in on-location work—city, land, seascapes—as well as annual reports.

Vlado Matisic
With a love of photography that developed from a hobby into a passion, Matisic is a traveller who captures the beauty of the landscape and the spirit of the countries he visits. Educated in Zagreb, Yugoslavia and London, England, he now freelances out of Vancouver.

William P. McElligott
Based in Ottawa, Ontario, this adventurous 36-year-old travels frequently—and sometimes dangerously—in his pursuit of images. His sharp eye for line and detail lends itself to his areas of specialty: advertising, architectural, aerial and sports photography.

Michael Morissette
Prior to his induction as photo coordinator for *The Expo Celebration*, Morissette led a comparatively normal life as the studio manager for Derik Murray Photography in Vancouver, B.C. He is a graduate of Ryerson Poly-technical Institute in Toronto, Ontario.

Patrick Morrow
Adventurer, author, producer, mountaineer, photo journalist. These are just a few of the credits for this remarkable 34-year-old British Columbian who has climbed the highest mountains on the world's seven continents. His photographs are published around the globe.

Derik Murray
Well-known commercial photographer Murray found *The Expo Celebration* a major departure from his usual fare. Although he could mention the many national and international awards to his credit, he'd rather talk about the time he showed Aborigine John Kalkurru how to use his camera.

Albert Normandin
The award-winning Normandin left town in 1982 for a three-year stint as assistant to Jay Maisel in New York City. Since returning to Vancouver as a freelance photographer, he's handled advertising, corporate, editorial and audio-visual assignments here and in the U.S.

Mike Paris
With a diverse education in economics and photography, the level-headed Paris spent seven years in retail advertising before opening P. S. Photography in 1982. His areas of specialty are illustrative and table-top photography. His special interest: underwater archaeology.

Simon Scott
Architectural photographer Scott has worked on a number of major projects for Arthur Erickson and Roloff Beny. His work as a photographer and designer has been published in Canada, the U.S., Japan, Britain, France and Italy. He lives and works in Vancouver.

Hans Sipma
The other half of Vancouver's P. S. Photography, Sipma is an accomplished advertising and editorial photographer as well as a TV director/cameraman. His portraits of Bryan Adams, Loverboy, Prism and Doug and the Slugs grace album jackets and magazines across North America.

Darryl Snaychuk
A dual resident of Edmonton and Vancouver, Snaychuk's brief history includes an early graduation from the Northern Alberta Institute of Technology's two-year photography program, two one-man exhibitions, a commercial apprenticeship and various freelance assignments.

Brian Stablyk
After graduating in Fine Arts from the University of British Columbia, Stablyk exhibited his work while completing a final year of graduate-level study in communications. Widely published, his portfolio features a Pacific Northwest stock library with over 100,000 images.

Norm Stelfox
Born and educated in Montreal, Stelfox made Vancouver his home in 1977. He is currently employed as a stock photographer and head of the Computer Science Department at Centennial Senior Secondary School in Coquitlam, B.C. His photos have appeared in many publications.

Lloyd Sutton
Sutton has a tendency to get a little wrapped up in his work, a characteristic he's put to excellent use on *The Expo Celebration*. Working as a freelance photographer for the past five years, he's travelled far and wide on tourism and industrial assignments.

Peter Timmermans
Once a teacher at the Bauhaus in Weimar, Timmermans was born in East Germany. He escaped to West Berlin, immigrating to Canada in 1979. He's only recently resumed his career in photography after working four years on the conceptual layout and design for EXPO 86.

Jürgen Vogt
Born in Berlin during the 1940's, Vogt moved to Canada in 1952. His first foray behind the lens was for *Time* in 1970. Since then he has covered Solidarity events in Poland and news from Italy, the U.S. and Canada. Today he works mostly on annual reports and audio-visuals.

Alex Waterhouse-Hayward
Waterhouse-Hayward was born in Buenos Aires, Argentina, in 1942. Prior to moving to Vancouver in 1975, he taught Ancient & Medieval History and Algebra in New Mexico. His first freelance assignment was shooting stills for Michael J. Fox's TV debut.

Jane Weitzel
Weitzel specializes in fashion advertising and personality portraits in her Vancouver studio. Her background includes work in Europe and as a medical photographer. For her, *The Expo Celebration* was an extension of what she enjoys best: meeting new faces every day.

Perry Zavitz
Born in the other London (Ontario), Zavitz followed his "somewhat normal childhood" with three years of formal photography training in the East and journeys to Paris and the American Midwest. He currently works as an advertising photographer in Vancouver.

The Producers of *The Expo Celebration* would also like to acknowledge the contributions of the following submission photographers and publications:
Carolyn Angus, John Bartosik, Peter Bregg, Barry Brooks, Thomas Bruckbauer, Mario Crudo, Brent Daniels, Jeffrey Devine, Victor Dezso, Alan Etkin, Rick Etkin, Chris Helcermanas Benge, Kent Kallberg, Cynthia Kanetsuka, Greg Kinch, Ed Long, Hugh Martell, Michael Mong, Marin Petkov, Michel Pilon, Cedric Poon, Colin Price, Tony Redpath, Mike Robertson, Martin Rowland, Gordon Schuck, Chris Speedie, Stephe Tate, Jeff Weddell, *Canadian Art, Canadian Living, Saturday Night*

CREATIVE TEAM &
ACKNOWLEDGEMENTS

Derik Murray
Creative Director

Marthe Love
Director of Operations

Michael Burch
Director of Marketing

Ray Hrynkow
Designer

David Grierson
Interviewer/Writer

Michael Morissette
Photography Coordinator

Darryl Snaychuk
Production Assistant

Elaine Jones
Text Editor

Robert Mitchell
Director of Sales

Eric Dahlberg
Sales Manager (Corporate)

Nancy Riesco Marchand
Production Assistant

Robert De Angelis
Comptroller

Casey Hrynkow
Design Consultant

Sheri Grierson
Text Editor

Judy Corvari
Production Assistant

We would like to extend a special thank you to the respective families of *The Expo Celebration* production team.

To produce a book the magnitude of *The Expo Celebration* required the assistance of many people. In particular, the management and staff of The Expo 86 Corporation were cooperative above and beyond the call of duty. To those not listed or inadvertently omitted we offer our hearty thanks. We would like to acknowledge the following people who helped make this project a success.

Agency Press
Rick Andrews
Jane Howard Baker
Diana Barkley
Mark Bitz
Gerry Blitstein
Lawrence Boxall
Constance Brissendon
Steve Brooks
Angus Brown
Geran Campbell
Bob Carey
John Carswell
Ian Carter
Bob Cherry
Bjarne Christensen
Gordon Clements
Wayne Collins
David Cooper
Mel Cooper
Carl Cundiff
Mike Cvitkovich
Mike Cyr
Ann Farris Darling
Allan Davidson
Myra Davies
Tracey Drebett
Larry Eaglestone
Bob English
Brent Esplen
Paula Fairweather
Bob Faulkner
Alfred Field
Don Finnie
Gail Flitten
Ann Garneau
Don Gee
Mark Germyn
Al Gray
Stuart Gear
Butch Greer
Keld Hansen
Bob Herger
Jaye Hornal
Jeff Hovey
Peter Hrynkow
Dave Jamieson
Judy Johnson
Michael Joss
George Kane
Peter Karlen
Robert Keziere
Theresa Kobayashi
Kodak Canada Ltd.

Koko Productions
Labatt's
Patricia La Nauze
Judy Larsen
The Lazy Gourmet
Ted Lea
Rhonda Legge
Jeff Lennard
Lens and Shutter
Leo's Cameras
Peter Little
Karen Love
Josanne Lovick
Rob Lucy
George McCarthy
Martha McCarthy
Robert McIlhargey
Jillian McInnes
Dawn Rae McLaren
Bill McMullen
George Madden
Peter Madliger
Man In Motion Staff
Vic Marks
Susan Mathieson
Ron Mayers
Michael Mead
Susan Mendelson
Walter Misa
Cameron Moore
Enrique Cedron Morales
Joseph Morrall
Jack Morris
Kathie Moseley
Bill Neill
Noel Newbolt
97 Kiss FM
George Ninkovich
John Nixon
Jill Nordstrom
Linda Oglov
Jim O'Hara
Jean Pierre Ollivier
Pacific Coast Staging
Michelle Paris
Kim Parton
Jim Pattison
Rick Peters
Art Phifer
Brad Philley
David Pilling
Glen Priest
Pat Puzzle
Quad Colour

Patrick Reid
George Roberts
Bob Rogers
Susan Rosenberg
Deborah Roitberg
Linda Roth
Pamela Ryan
Darlene Sanders
Ullrich Schade
Alice Schlenker
Simons Advertising
Slicko Studios
Charlie Smith
Marlene Solberg
Wendy Soobis
Bonnie Spence
Kathi Springer
Randy Squires
Glenys Stewart
Harvey Stone
Bruce Streigler
Ann Tanner
Brad Thompson
John Thompson
Terry Trapnell
Karen Tripp
The Typeworks
Jerry Volny
Ron Walsh
Lee Watson
Catherine Wells
Wes Wenhardt
Brenda Lea White
Paul Williams
Trisha Williamson
Ron Woodall
Zenith Graphics

Special thanks to Margaret Watson of Cantel and to David Brekke of Jim Pattison Cellular for keeping the lines of communication open.

Extra special thanks to the visitors to EXPO 86 for taking the precious time to talk with us, pose for photographs, and for simply coming to the Exposition.